THE BEST OF
BESTON

THE BEST OF
BESTON

A Selection from the Natural World of

HENRY BESTON

from Cape Cod

to the

St. Lawrence

Edited and Introduced by

ELIZABETH COATSWORTH

A Nonpareil Book

DAVID R. GODINE · PUBLISHER · BOSTON

First softcover edition, including new photographs, published by

NONPAREIL BOOKS
David R. Godine, Publisher, Inc.
P. O. BOX 450, JAFFREY, NEW HAMPSHIRE 03452

Library of Congress Cataloging-in-Publication Data
Beston, Henry, 1888–1968
[Especially Maine]
The best of Beston: a selection from the natural world of Henry Beston from
Cape Cod to the St. Lawrence / edited and introduced by Elizabeth Coatsworth.
p. cm. — (A Nonpareil book)
Originally published: Especially Maine. Brattleboro, Vt. S. Greene Press, 1970.
ISBN: 1-56792-104-3 (alk. paper)
1. Natural history — New England. I. Coatsworth, Elizabeth Jane, 1893–
II. Title. III. Series.

QH104.5.N4B48   2000
508.74 — dc21
00 — 29372

Printed in the United States of America

Contents

SOUTH OF MAINE

IN MAINE

NORTH OF MAINE

I wish here to give my warm thanks to Janet Greene, to whose editorial skill this book owes its final shape and proportions. My gratitude is also due my sister Margaret for allowing me to use parts of some of the letters H.B. wrote to her, her husband, and our mother over the years; and to Dr. Luther Neff and Mr. David McCord, who have permitted the use of pertinent material from Henry's correspondence with them.

ELIZABETH BESTON

THE BEST OF
BESTON

La Nature, voilà mon pays.
L'oeuvre—célébrer, révéler la mystère, la beauté,
et la mystique de la Nature, du Monde Visible.
Attacher ce sentiment à mon nom.

[Inscribed on the inside cover of the first of his notebooks for *The Outermost House*, dated in December 1926. It was the dedication of himself as a writer-naturalist, the phrase he was hereafter always to use. E.C.B.]

Foreword

When in the mid-Twenties Henry came to live on the great beach at Eastham on the outer Cape he was thirty-six or thirty-seven years old and had already written five or six books.

Of these he thought very little. Two were about the first World War in France and on the sea. The earlier, *Volunteer Poilu*, he had signed "Henry Sheahan," his own name; but after that he used "Beston," his middle name, given him for his grandmother's family, tentatively signing *Full Speed Ahead* "Henry B. Beston," and then dropping the meaningless "B." Both these books Henry considered journalism.

For two books of fairy tales, written in the seventeenth-century Parson Capen house at Topsfield, north of Boston, he had some affection. They had been written to get the war out of his mind, he used to say. But there were weak spots in the writing and several stories or parts of stories were left out when at the farm in 1952 he revised his *Firelight Fairy Book* and *Starlight Wonder Book* into a single volume, *Henry Beston's Fairy Tales*. The *Book of Gallant Vagabonds* was written largely in a hotel room in New York, during two winters. The lives of Ledyard, Belzoni, Trelawney, Morton of Merrymount, James Bruce and Rimbaud

1

are all interesting, but it was a book written from books, and Henry used to say of it, "When I wrote that, I knew very little about life." A small story for children, *The Sons of Kai*, re-told a Navajo legend and marked a long winter visit with a friend in New Mexico.

But none of those books came up to Henry's exacting stand-ards. They were practice for his pen, as was his editorship of *The Living Age*, a monthly miscellany of British, French and German articles published at the Atlantic Monthly office. Henry had a remarkable memory. By the time he came to the Cape, it was well stocked on many subjects, including the writings of W. H. Hudson, Thoreau, Tomlinson, Conrad, and Jefferies, whom I name last because it was his work that Henry most admired. He never liked to have *The Outermost House* com-pared to Thoreau's *Cape Cod*. "Thoreau had very little heart," he would say.

A man's thirties are often called the prime of life, and Henry's Cape Cod years lay in this halcyon period. He was tall, hand-some, engaging and often very amusing. No one who ever heard him sing chanties to his accordion on the steps of the Fo'castle or indoors by the open fire would forget the charm of the ex-perience. He had a fine voice, whether speaking or singing, and though he was no musician and played mostly by ear, he could make the accordion or some out-of-tune old upright piano sing under his fingers.

Sometimes he drew small pictures of seashore and dunes, or of hills. They were drawn with only a few lines, but they gave an astonishing sense of space and of the rhythm of natural forms. This gift, too, he decried as "something to amuse the ladies," and seldom used.

He took a sporadic interest in his appearance and was very independent about how he dressed. His tweed jackets were made to order in London. Usually he wore a French dark blue beret. His shoes were casual and unconstricting; he liked wool

ties, and viyella shirts, of scarlet or glowing yellow with bishop sleeves, often worn with an Indian vest instead of a jacket; he was one of the first to wear walking shorts. But Henry had a sense of occasion and could dress formally for formal appearances. Whether dressed in his best or in an old shirt and shorts with bare feet, he was equally at his ease.

It was on the dunes that he found himself as a writer. There he was alone most of the time with only the sea, the sky, the beach and the marshes for company. He watched the seasons come and go on this vast stage. For the first time, he had a house of his own. He needed to possess and be possessed by his surroundings. He needed to brood, uninterrupted, for as long as he wished. He needed to observe at leisure. Lastly, he needed to write when he was ready to write, mostly in the mornings, his best time, though he put down notes at any hour.

At the Fo'castle he observed carefully, brooded long, and wrote slowly at the sturdy kitchen table overlooking the west and the great Eastham marshes. He wrote with a pencil or pen—on typewriter paper, except when taking notes—he never typed, for the sound of a machine would have interfered with the rhythm of his sentences, which meant so much to him. As he worked, the floor became littered with sheets of discarded paper. He sometimes spent an entire morning on a single sentence, unable to go on until he was completely satisfied with both words and cadence, which he considered equally important.

At the Maine farm, where all his later books were written, he followed this same routine of long preparation and slow writing, wrestling when necessary with a recalcitrant word, and then perhaps picking up speed again. Whether working in the study halfway down the hayfield above the pond, or, more often, in the herb attic, there was always a kitchen table, a strong uncushioned chair, a mug filled with sharpened pencils, a large eraser and a pile of typewriter paper, more than half of which ended life on the floor.

At the Fo'castle there were, of course, necessary interruptions to his work, when he might walk the beach to gather driftwood, or once or twice a week go to the lifesaving station where a taxi would meet him to take him to town for his shopping. His purchases were limited to what he could carry back in his knapsack on the return trip of almost two miles along the beach.

He also had his meals to cook. His cooking was simple— mostly macaroni and cheese, noodles, baked beans, Indian pudding or corn bread, and now and then batches of popovers that never rose—but were always flavored perfectly. He added some fruit and milk to balance this starchy diet, which kept him in excellent health. His only refrigerator was a small shelf built at the porch corner, high up out of reach of animals.

After *The Outermost House* was published and Henry and I were married, we lived in Hingham overlooking the harbor near Boston. Henry did not like this life with its grind of passing cars and its quality of an old South Shore village slowly turning into a suburb. We often went back to the Cape for a fortnight or a month or a few days, sometimes at the Fo'castle, sometimes at Mrs. Kelley's boardinghouse in Eastham, sometimes in a house we might rent on the marshes or on a back road. Once we stayed for a chilly spring fortnight in a little cottage on one of the ponds that speckle the Cape. At this time, Henry thought of writing a book on the inland cape. He finished a fine chapter on eeling at Eastham Salt Pond and part of another chapter on the marshes, but he was ruthless with his own work. He refused to write a minor book about the country of which he had written what he was sure from the first was a classic, and so tore up all he had begun.

Already at this time Henry had many ties with Maine. He used to visit at Sutton's Island off Northeast Harbor on Mt. Desert, and cruise along the coast among its islands and innumerable small harbors. He also visited in Damariscotta, the birthplace to which his friend Maurice Day and his wife Bee had returned with their two little boys, one of whom had Beston as his middle name. Jake, as everyone calls Maurice, had illus-

5

trated Henry's fairy tales when the Days were living near Boston. They had become close friends, and a year after the birth of our elder daughter, Henry was visiting Jake on his new houseboat, the Ark, which floated on Damariscotta Pond at the end of Deep Cove, almost hidden between folds of unspoiled forest.

It was on this visit that Henry heard of a farm for sale on the Neck, as peninsulas are called in this part of the country.

Jake told him that the farm's woodlot partly enclosed Deep Cove. This was enough for Henry. Without more than a passing glimpse of the house, he decided to buy the place. He who might hesitate for hours on the choice of a few words, could make up his mind on the future course of his life in an instant.

Once back in Hingham Henry took me out for lunch in Quincy. I remember that we ordered fish sticks (for Henry haddock was the only fish that existed).

"How would you like to have us buy a Maine farm?" he asked at the end of the meal, and I said, also in a split second, "It sounds fine."

A few weeks later we bought the farm. We never looked at any other piece of property. Perhaps it was fortunate that the next spring I was busy having our second daughter, for this gave Henry a chance to grow into the farm during his visits to superintend the repairs. The only running water came from a pump in the kitchen. He put in plumbing and a bathroom, changed the windows back to the original twelve panes—the house had been built sometime about 1835—repainted the faded yellow a strong farmhouse red, built an open porch between the dining room and the kitchen ell, which he painted white for the sake of variation, and then oversaw the indoor painting and papering and bought the necessary furniture.

In these matters my advice was asked, but it was Henry who was on the spot to make the final decisions, who talked with carpenters, masons and painters—and liked them all—who looked up to see a deer and a doe standing in the rocky pasture above the hayfield.

This was not like the solitary splendor of the Great Beach, but it had its own rural beauty and the year passed across it with its own different pageantry. It was a new and exciting experience to Henry, and once again he possessed and was possessed. When we had moved to the farm he seldom returned to the Cape. If he felt like going anywhere, we usually headed northward to Quebec and the French Canadian villages on the St. Lawrence.

One day Morris Rubin of Senator La Follette's *Progressive* came to see Henry and talked with him late into the evening by the open fire in the kitchen. During this talk Henry agreed to do a weekly Country Chronicle for the paper and from these columns later put together *Northern Farm*, with delightful illustrations by the Canadian artist Thoreau Macdonald, who felt as poetically as did Henry on all country matters. As always he wrote well when he wrote from himself.

The same was true of *Herbs and the Earth*. Henry started a ten-foot herb border along one edge of what we called the Court, although it was open on the east facing an old apple tree and the pond beyond. First, he spent long hours with catalogues and at herb-raising greenhouses, choosing the plants. When the bed was planted, Henry, dressed in his oldest working clothes, would go out to sit beside the border staring down at it. At long intervals he might crumble a piece of earth between his fingers, or pull up a weed. But mostly he was just staring and staring. When he came in, he would say, "I've been working in the herb garden all morning." It might indeed be the man-of-all-work who had spaded and planted and weeded, but in a truer sense Henry *would* have been working even harder in the herb garden, pondering the meaning of the earth between his fingers and the fragrant leaves about him. In fact Lawrence or Ellis or whoever was with us, had become a part of Henry. He himself would have found it hard to say which man had done what in the garden or on the place.

Out of these hours *Herbs and the Earth* was born. Henry

7

considered the last passages in this book the best he had ever written.

At various times during these years at the farm Henry collected two anthologies. In 1937 *American Memory* was published from firsthand accounts of American life from the early explorers down to 1925. Some years later, in 1950, appeared *White Pine and Blue Water*, using only Maine material. Both these books were put together in the big herb attic under the dormer window which Henry had had built to hold his table and chair. With his remarkable memory and literary taste, the choice of materials was not difficult. He sent to the Boston Athenaeum and the Maine State Library for books, but in general he knew just what he wanted and made quick decisions.

Then, as usual, his own introductions to the sections were a slow, grinding business. The remarkable thing is that his writing always seemed inevitable when it was finished. He kept it fresh, however long he might work upon it.

A far more important book was *The St. Lawrence* for The Rivers of America series. Again, this was something he felt ready to undertake. We had already often driven to Quebec and the St. Lawrence villages. He had watched the river in many lights, but now he went about observing it more closely. "I don't want this to be just history," he said. "It must be primarily about the river itself." And most of the next months he spent in living the life of the St. Lawrence. For part of the summer he rented a cottage for the whole family beyond Murray Bay. He took, of course, the Saguenay trip and also sailed up the St. Lawrence and into Lake Ontario as far as Toronto, coming back through the La Chine rapids. On another trip on a little coastal half-cargo, half-passenger steamer, he left Quebec and went down the river and through the Straits of Belle Isle into the open Atlantic, stopping at ports in Newfoundland and Labrador. Once he hired a tippy, tug-like boat a little beyond the Saguenay, where at that time the road along the north shore of the river stopped. The destination was the Indian village of Bersimis, forty miles downriver, where the priest gave us lodgings, and the chief tried to present Henry with a pair of bear cubs as we were leaving. Later, in the cold, stormy autumn, he took a boat carrying lumbermen to one of the lumber camps on the north shore of the lower river. He got on well with all types of French Canadians. His mother had come from Paris, and the French Canadians admired his pronunciation and his good humor. Again alone, he drove along the south shore of the river to the Gaspé. Of course, he wrote about history, too, but through it all the great living river flows.

The St. Lawrence was the last country outside of Maine that he felt like writing about.

He already knew many parts of France, Italy, Ireland, and Spain, which he loved for the courtesy of its people. During our marriage we traveled in England, Yucatán and elsewhere in Mexico. We rode horses on Arizona dude ranches. We stayed for part of many winters in California. All these things he enjoyed, but they were outside him. He never wrote or would write a word about them, except for the necessary references to France and Ireland in his early war books; each of these countries was half of his inheritance, but he never wanted to go back to them. He saw most places with his eyes, not with his heart, and only when he had become part of a landscape could he write about it with what the Romans would have called filial piety.

Perhaps Henry's great gift was to call attention to things that had always been there, but whose significance had gone largely unnoticed until he spoke or wrote about them.

He was a great opener of windows.

SOUTH OF MAINE

About the Outermost House

Around 1925 Henry bought dune land at Eastham on the outer Cape on which he had a house built by the local boss carpenter, Harvey Moore. It was small, strong and exactly what he wanted. Others might call it a cottage, a cabin or even a shack. Henry called it a house. It had one room with an entryway where his oilskins and lantern hung. There was a narrow extra room to the north with a cot, bureau and hooks for clothes.

But essentially the Fo'castle, as it was always called in the beginning, consisted of a single room. It was simple and functional, with a brick fireplace on the north, a folding bed under the east windows facing the sea, a small oil cookstove set into a shelf between the china cupboard and Red Jacket (the pump) on the south, and a kitchen table beneath the west windows looking out on the great Eastham marshes and the far-off outline of the village.

It is perhaps a curious fact that he who saw, heard, smelled and felt so much more of the natural world about him than do most others, was to some degree handicapped. In the first place, he was nearsighted. His old-fashioned steel- or gold-rimmed glasses were usually in his left-hand breast pocket.

"They make the world too much like a publicity photograph,"

he would say. "When I don't use them everything seems more beautiful, like a tapestry."

He was also a little deaf, even at this time. The babble of a room filled with people confused him. In talking with one person he usually sat with his "good ear" toward the speaker. Yet distant sounds, like an approaching train or car or a far-off shot, he heard before anyone else. Perhaps, too, he could distinguish the component sounds of a breaking wave more clearly than others might.

His handicaps never seemed of any importance. He knew exactly what he wanted to see or hear, and he saw and heard it, with the aid of eyeglasses, bird glasses, or by his power of concentration. He was acutely conscious of the movements of the air about him, of the changes in the sounds of leaves from spring to fall, of odors ("j'aime toutes les odeurs, même les mauvaises," as he used to quote with relish). Above all, he watched the sky with its clouds by day and its stars by night. He often went out before dawn to see a planet rise from the ocean or a constellation make its first seasonal appearance. He knew and loved them all, especially Orion, and many years later, when he was old, this love of the night sky was his final and strongest bond with the earth he had celebrated.

From the beginning, he was certain that *The Outermost House* was really good, as he felt that none of his earlier books had been. He had put the best of himself into it and until the day of his death forty years later, he was proud of it. When it was published the reviews were few, the sales only adequate, but he never lost faith in its ultimate survival. Sometimes for a few months it would be out of print, but year after year new editions were brought out. In 1953 a French paperback appeared (*Une Maison au Bout du Monde*). "It's better in French than in English," he exclaimed, pleased and amused, when he had finished reading it.

14

Meanwhile, recognition was coming. Henry was given honorary degrees by Bowdoin College and the University of Maine. In 1949 Harvard made him an honorary member of Phi Beta Kappa. In 1954 he was elected to the Boston branch of the American Academy of Arts and Sciences and awarded the Emerson-Thoreau Medal. All these honors brought him great pleasure, more for the sake of *The Outermost House*, perhaps, than for himself.

Then in 1964 came the final honor at the very moment when it could give him most happiness, for even by the next year he could not have gone to Cape Cod, nor spoken publicly. But the honor came in time, so that he lived his final years knowing that his work had been truly recognized. Some time before this he had given the Fo'castle and its dunes, sadly diminished by wind and tide, to the Massachusetts Audubon Society.

Now the Outermost House, as it had come to be called, was made a National Literary Landmark, with a bronze plaque on its weathered shingles, which read:

"The Outermost House in which Henry Beston, Author-Naturalist, wrote his classic book by that name wherein he sought the great truth and found it in the nature of man.

"This plaque dedicated October 11, 1964, by a grateful citizenry, at a ceremony denoting the Outermost House a National Literary Monument.

"Endicott Peabody
Governor of Massachusetts

"Stewart L. Udall
Secretary of the Interior

"The Massachusetts Audubon Society."

I think the idea for this occasion may have originated with the governor's wife, Mrs. Peabody, and Ivan Sandrof, a Worces-

15

ter critic and newspaperman, but everyone pitched in to make it a great celebration. After a lobster luncheon we were driven out to the slope of the dunes below what had been the lifesaving station. There were seats for perhaps a hundred people in a natural amphitheater of sand. The speakers sat on a platform protected by a low wall. Beyond, above and to each side of this screen lay the everlasting sea, bright in the sunshine and whipped to whitecaps by the October wind. There were four or five speeches and Henry gave a few words in response. ("He won't be able to make his voice heard," I said to the technician in charge of the amplifiers. "When I get through, he'll be heard in Spain," the man said cheerfully.)

Henry's voice was not heard in Spain, but it was heard by all the crowd which so warmly and lovingly faced him. Then we were taken in a beach-buggy to the Outermost House on what was to be his last visit there. The little house had been twice moved, once because a gale had washed away the sand to its very steps; a second time because the wind had hollowed out the dune beneath the building so that it was about to collapse into the cavity. Now in its third position it nestles like a partridge close to the marsh. Its old pride, facing the sea from the very crest of a high dune, is gone forever. During this last move, the fireplace was not brought with it, and now it is warmed only by a stove.

But to Henry this was as it should be. "Creation is here and now," he had written. Dunes might come and go, and so might men and women, but now he felt that his work had achieved its destined place, and he was satisfied.

16

THE OUTERMOST HOUSE

[Letter to Miss Elizabeth Coatsworth]

The Fo'castle

Lat. 41° 51' 39" N.

Long. 69° 57' 08" W.

Haven't been anywhere, haven't seen anybody, and only one
guest over the 4th, Corey Ford of Vanity Fair. He brought me a
poison arrow case—a beautifully carved bamboo affair—from
the headwaters of some river in Dutch Borneo. Then to papers
and pencils again. The book is about ⅔ done; would Zeus it
were more. Though I have a world of joy in doing it, in polishing
rhythms, in choosing adjectives which know what I mean—it's
been a long pull since Feb. 1, nay, since Jan. 1, endlessly shaping,
retouching, working. My last chapter was on "Night on the
Great Beach" and I let myself go, for there's a soupçon of the
noctambule in me; or—the noctamorist, I love night. By day
space belongs to man, it is his sun that is shining, his clouds
that are floating past; by night, space is his no more. He escapes,
then, from his own world into the universe. Night in midocean,
with the lights out, the mast and the rigging swaying against
stars—that's night at its best, most awesome, heaviest with
beauty. Dune nights are very beautiful too. A real northern
night—north Canada, north Norway—voilà something I'd like
to see. I know tropical and West Indian nights.

17

*Now, D.V., I go on to a study of waves. No one has ever
written a real study of the shapes and colors and tricks of
waves. One of those read or skip but gol-darn-you-if-you-do-skip
chapters. The midsummer chapter is done, hot and heavy with
sun on the dunes, sun holding the sand in place, the air full of
a good smell of ocean vegetation drying in the sun.*

[From "The Beach"]

The great rhythms of nature, today so dully disregarded,
wounded even, have here their spacious and primeval liberty;
cloud and shadow of cloud, wind and tide, tremor of night and
day. Journeying birds alight here and fly away again all unseen,
schools of fish move beneath the waves, the surf flings its spray
against the sun.

[From "Autumn, Ocean, and Birds"]

We need another and wiser and perhaps a more mystical concept of animals. Remote from universal nature, and living by
complicated artifice, man in civilization surveys the creature
through the glass of his knowledge and sees thereby a feather
magnified and the whole image in distortion. We patronize them
for their incompleteness, for their tragic fate of having taken
form so far below ourselves. And therein we err, and greatly
err. For the animal shall not be measured by man. In a world
older and more complete than ours they move finished and
complete, gifted with extensions of the senses we have lost or
never attained, living by voices we shall never hear. They are
not brethren, they are not underlings; they are other nations,
caught with ourselves in the net of life and time, fellow prisoners
of the splendor and travail of the earth.

18

[From "The Headlong Wave"]

They say here that great waves reach this coast in threes. Three great waves, then an indeterminate run of lesser rhythms, then three great waves again. On Celtic coasts it is the seventh wave that is seen coming like a king out of the grey, cold sea. The Cape tradition, however, is no half-real, half-mystical fancy, but the truth itself. Great waves do indeed approach this beach by threes. Again and again have I watched three giants roll in one after the other out of the Atlantic, cross the outer bar, break, form again, and follow each other in to fulfillment and destruction on this solitary beach. Coast Guard crews are all well aware of this triple rhythm and take advantage of the lull that follows the last wave to launch their boats.

It is true that there are single giants as well. I have been roused by them in the night. Waked by their tremendous and unexpected crash, I have sometimes heard the last of the heavy overspill, sometimes only the loud, withdrawing roar. After the roar came a briefest pause, and after the pause the return of ocean to the night's long cadences. Such solitary titans, flinging their green tons down upon a quiet world, shake beach and dune. Late one September night, as I sat reading, the very father of all waves must have flung himself down before the house, for the quiet of the night was suddenly overturned by a gigantic, tumbling crash and an earthquake rumbling; the beach trembled beneath the avalanche, the dune shook, and my house so shook on its dune that the flame of a lamp quivered and pictures jarred on the wall.

The three great elemental sounds in nature are the sound of rain, the sound of wind in a primeval wood, and the sound of outer ocean on a beach. I have heard them all, and of the three elemental voices, that of ocean is the most awesome, beautiful, and varied. For it is a mistake to talk of the monotone of ocean or of the monotonous nature of its sound. The sea has

19

many voices. Listen to the surf, really lend it your ears, and you will hear in it a world of sounds: hollow boomings and heavy roarings, great watery tumblings and tramplings, long hissing seethes, sharp, rifle-shot reports, splashes, whispers, the grinding undertone of stones, and sometimes vocal sounds that might be the half-heard talk of people in the sea. And not only is the great sound varied in the manner of its making, it is also constantly changing its tempo, its pitch, its accent, and its rhythm, being now loud and thundering, now almost placid, now furious, now grave and solemn-slow, now a simple measure, now a rhythm monstrous with a sense of purpose and elemental will.

Every mood of the wind, every change in the day's weather, every phase of the tide—all these have subtle sea musics all their own. Surf of the ebb, for instance, is one music, surf of the flood another, the change in the two musics being most clearly marked during the first hour of a rising tide. With the renewal of the tidal energy, the sound of the surf grows louder, the fury of battle returns to it as it turns again on the land, and beat and sound change with the renewal of the war.

Sound of surf in these autumnal dunes—the continuousness of it, sound of endless charging, endless incoming and gathering, endless fulfillment and dissolution, endless fecundity, and end-less death. I have been trying to study out the mechanics of that mighty resonance. The dominant note is the great spilling crash made by each arriving wave. It may be hollow and boom-ing, it may be heavy and churning, it may be a tumbling roar. The second fundamental sound is the wild seething cataract roar of the wave's dissolution and the rush of its foaming waters up the beach—this second sound *diminuendo*. The third funda-mental sound is the endless dissolving hiss of the inmost slides of foam. The first two sounds reach the ear as a unisonance—the booming impact of the tons of water and the wild roar of the uprush blending—and this mingled sound dissolves into the foam-bubble hissing of the third. Above the tumult, like birds, fly wisps of watery noise, splashes and countersplashes, whispers, seethings, slaps, and chucklings. An overtone sound of other breakers, mingled with a general rumbling, fills earth and sea and air.

Here do I pause to warn my reader that although I have recounted the history of a breaker—an ideal breaker—the surf process must be understood as mingled and continuous, waves hurrying after waves, interrupting waves, washing back on waves, overwhelming waves. Moreover, I have described the sound of a high surf in fair weather. A storm surf is mechanically the same thing, but it *grinds*, and this same long, sepulchral grinding—sound of utter terror to all mariners—is a development of the second fundamental sound; it is the cry of the breaker water roaring its way ashore and dragging at the sand. A strange underbody of sound when heard through the high, wild screaming of a gale.

Breaking waves that have to run up a steep tilt of the beach are often followed by a dragging, grinding sound—the note of the baffled water running downhill again to the sea. It is loudest when the tide is low and breakers are rolling beach stones up and down a slope of the lower beach.

I am, perhaps, most conscious of the sound of surf just after I have gone to bed. Even here I read myself to drowsiness, and, reading, I hear the cadenced trampling roar filling all the dark. So close is the Fo'castle to the ocean's edge that the rhythm of sound I hear oftenest in fair weather is not so much a general tumult as an endless arrival, overspill, and dissolution of separate great seas. Through the dark, mathematic square of the screened half-window, I listen to the rushes and the bursts, the tramplings, and the long, intermingled thunderings, never wearying of the sonorous and universal sound.

Away from the beach, the various sounds of the surf melt

21

into one great thundering symphonic roar. Autumnal nights in Eastham village are full of this ocean sound. The "summer people" have gone, the village rests and prepares for winter, lamps shine from kitchen windows, and from across the moors, the great levels of the marsh, and the bulwark of the dunes resounds the long wintry roaring of the sea. Listen to it awhile, and it will seem but one remote and formidable sound; listen still longer and you will discern in it a symphony of breaker thunderings, an endless, distant, elemental cannonade. There is beauty in it, and ancient terror. I heard it last as I walked through the village on a starry October night; there was no wind, the leafless trees were still, all the village was abed, and the whole somber world was awesome with the sound.

Blowing all day long, a northwest wind yesterday swept the sky clear of every tatter and wisp of cloud. Clear it still is, though the wind has shifted to the east. The sky this afternoon is a harmony of universal blue, bordered with a surf rim of snowiest blue-white. Far out at sea, in the northeast and near the horizon, is a pool of the loveliest blue I have ever seen here—a light blue, a petal blue, blue of the emperor's gown in a Chinese fairy tale. If you would see waves at their best, come on such a day, when the ocean reflects a lovely sky, and the wind is light and onshore; plan to arrive in the afternoon so that you will have the sun facing the breakers. Come early, for the glints on the waves are most beautiful and interesting when the light is oblique and high. And come with a rising tide.

The surf is high, and on the far side of it, a wave greater than its fellows is shouldering out of the blue, glinting immensity of sea.

Friends tell me that there are certain tropic beaches where waves miles long break all at once in one cannonading crash: a little of this, I imagine, would be magnificent; a constancy of it,

22

unbearable. The surf here is broken; it approaches the beach in long intercurrent parallels, some a few hundred feet long, some an eighth of a mile long, some, and the longest, attaining the quarter-mile length and perhaps just over. Thus, at all times and instants of the day, along the five miles of beach visible from the Fo'castle deck, waves are to be seen breaking, coursing in to break, seething up and sliding back.

But to return to the blue wave rolling in out of the blue spaciousness of sea. On the other side of the world, just opposite the Cape, lies the ancient Spanish province of Galicia, and the town of Pontevedra and St. James Compostella, renowned of pilgrims. (When I was there they offered me a silver cockle shell, but I would have none of it, and got myself a sea shell from some Galician fisher-folk.) Somewhere between this Spanish land and Cape Cod the pulse of earth has engendered this wave and sent it coursing westward through the seas. Far off the coast, the spray of its passing has, perhaps, risen on the windward bow of some rusty freighter and fallen in rainbow drops upon her plates; the great liners have felt it course beneath their keels.

A continent rises in the west, and the pulse beat approaches this bulwark of Cape Cod. Two thirds of a mile out, the wave is still a sea vibration, a billow. Slice it across, and its outline will be that of a slightly flattened semicircle; the pulse is shaped in a long, advancing mound. I watch it approach the beach. Closer and closer in, it is rising with the rise of the beach and the shoaling of the water; closer still, it is changing from a mound to a pyramid, a pyramid which swiftly distorts, the seaward side lengthening, the landward side incurving—the wave is now a breaker. Along the ridge of blue forms a rippling crest of clear, bright water, a little spray flies off. Under the racing foam churned up by the dissolution of other breakers the beach now catches at the last shape of sea inhabited by the pulse—the wave

23

is *tripped* by the shoaling sand—the giant stumbles, crashes, and is pushed over and ahead by the sloping line of force behind. The fall of a breaker is never the work of gravity alone.

It is the last line of the wave that has captured the decorative imagination of the world—the long seaward slope, the curling crest, the incurved volute ahead.

Toppling over and hurled ahead, the wave crashes, its mass of glinting blue falling down in a confusion of seething, splendid white, the tumbling water rebounding from the sand to a height always a little above that of the original crest. Out of the wild, crumbling confusion born of the dissolution of the force and the last great shape, foamy fountains spurt, and ringlets of spray. The mass of water, still all furiously a-churn and seething white, now rushes for the rim of the beach as it might for an inconceivable cataract. Within thirty-five feet the water shoals from two feet to dry land. The edge of the rush thins, and the last impulse disappears in inch-deep slides of foam which reflect the sky in one last moment of energy and beauty and then vanish all at once into the sands.

Another thundering, and the water that has escaped and withdrawn is gathered up and swept forward again by another breaking wave. Night and day, age after age, so works the sea, with infinite variation obeying an unalterable rhythm moving through an intricacy of chance and law.

[From "Midwinter"]

A year indoors is a journey along a paper calendar; a year in outer nature is the accomplishment of a tremendous ritual. To share in it, one must have a knowledge of the pilgrimages of the sun, and something of that natural sense of him and feeling for him which made even the most primitive people mark the summer limits of his advance and the last December ebb of his decline. All these autumn weeks I have watched the great disk going south along the horizon of moorlands beyond the marsh, now sinking behind this field, now behind this leafless tree, now behind this sedgy hillock dappled with thin snow. We lose a great deal, I think, when we lose this sense and feeling for the sun. When all has been said, the adventure of the sun is the great natural drama by which we live, and not to have joy in it and awe of it, not to share in it, is to close a dull door on Nature's sustaining and poetic spirit.

Animal life has disappeared into the chill air, the heavy, lifeless sand. On the surface, nothing remains of the insect world. That multiplicity of insect tracks, those fantastic ribbons which grasshoppers, promenading flies, spiders, and beetles printed on the dunes as they went about their hungry and mysterious purposes, have come to an end in this world and left it all the poorer. Those trillions of unaccountable lives, those crawling, buzzing, intense presences which nature created to fulfill some unknown purpose or perhaps simply to satisfy a whim for a certain sound or a moment of exquisite color, where are they now, in this vast world, silent save for the somber thunder of the surf and the rumble of wind in the porches of the ears?

As I muse here, it occurs to me that we are not sufficiently grateful for the great symphony of natural sound which insects add to the natural scene; indeed, we take it so much as a matter of course that it does not stir our fully conscious attention. But all those little fiddles in the grass, all those cricket pipes, those delicate flutes, are they not lovely beyond words when heard in midsummer on a moonlight night? I like, too, the movement they give to a landscape with their rushes, their strange comings and goings, and their hoverings with the sun's brilliance reflected

25

in their wings. Here, and at this especial moment, there is no trace or vestige of the summer's insect world, yet one feels them here, the trillion, trillion tiny eggs in grass and marsh and sand, all faithfully sealed and hidden away, all waiting for the rush of this earth through space and the resurgence of the sun.

[From "Winter Visitors"]

It is not good to be too much alone, even as it is unwise to be always with and in a crowd, but, solitary as I was, I had few opportunities for moods or to "lose and neglect the creeping hours of time." From the moment that I rose in the morning and threw open my door looking toward the sea to the moment when the spurt of a match sounded in the evening quiet of my solitary house, there was always something to do, something to observe, something to record, something to study, something to put aside in a corner of the mind. There was the ocean in all weathers and at all tides, now grey and lonely and veiled in winter rain, now sun-bright, coldly green, and marbled with dissolving foam; there was the marsh with its great congresses, its little companies, its wandering groups, and little family gatherings of winter birds; there was the glory of the winter sky rolling out of the ocean over and across the dunes, constellation by constellation, lonely star by star. To see the night sky in all its divinity of beauty, the world beneath it should be lovely, too, else the great picture is split in halves which no mind can ever really weld into a unity of reverence.

I think the nights on which I felt most alone (if I paused to indulge myself in such an emotion) were the nights when southeasterly rains were at work in the dark, immense world outside my door, dissolving in rain and fog such ice and snow as lingered on after a snowfall or a cold spell had become history. On such southeasterly nights, the fog lay thick on marsh and ocean, the distant lights of Eastham vanished in a universal dark, and on the invisible beach below the dune, great breakers born of fog-swell and the wind rolled up the sands with the slow, mournful pace of stately victims destined to immolation, and toppled over, each one, in a heavy, awesome roar that faded to silence before a fellow victim followed on out of the darkness on the sea. Only one sense impression lingered to remind me of the vanished world of man, and that the long, long complaints and melancholy bellowings of vessels feeling their way about, miles offshore.

[To Miss Coatsworth]

You know Klah, the Navaho medicine man—he asked me for some Cape Cod sea sand a year or two ago, for he wanted to do some particularly aquarian magic. Rather a curious thing happened. I turned in one pleasant night saying to myself as I climbed in, "I'll get that sand at sunrise in the morning; I'll gather it ritually at the ritual hour." Well—all that night a S.E. wind blew, blowing the very finest topsand, the very purest, wind-sifted sand, into the crevice between the floor of the beach and the wall of the dunes. When I came down in the morning there was a run of this sand lying in the angle like clean snow on a threshold up against a door. Quite, quite a different sand. I had a box with me. The sky was glorious and cloudless, pure space, the east a true rose, the ocean solemn and darker than the sky. A yellow crescent at the horizon—neither the words "yellow" or "gold" or any word will give that burning edge—and I began to gather the sand in clean hands and pour it into the box. Oh, if you had only been there—you, the one person in the world who would have completely and joyously understood.

27

[From "An Inland Stroll in Spring"]

Into every empty corner, into all forgotten things and nooks, Nature struggles to pour life, pouring life into the dead, into life itself. That immense, overwhelming, relentless, burning ardency of Nature for the stir of life!

[From "Night on the Great Beach"]

Our fantastic civilization has fallen out of touch with many aspects of nature, and with none more completely than with night. Primitive folk, gathered at a cave mouth round a fire, do not fear night; they fear, rather, the energies and creatures to whom night gives power; we of the age of the machines, having delivered ourselves of nocturnal enemies, now have a dislike of night itself. With lights and ever more lights, we drive the holiness and beauty of night back to the forests and the sea; the little villages, the crossroads even, will have none of it. Are modern folk, perhaps, afraid of night? Do they fear that vast serenity, the mystery of infinite space, the austerity of stars? Having made themselves at home in a civilization obsessed with power, which explains its whole world in terms of energy, do they fear at night for their dull acquiescence and the pattern of their beliefs? Be the answer what it will, today's civilization is full of people who will have not the slightest notion of the character or the poetry of night, who have never even seen night. Yet to live thus, to know only artificial night, is as absurd and evil as to know only artificial day.

Night is very beautiful on this great beach. It is the true other half of the day's tremendous wheel; no lights without meaning stab or trouble it; it is beauty, it is fulfillment, it is rest. Thin clouds float in these heavens, islands of obscurity in a splendor of space and stars: the Milky Way bridges earth and ocean; the

28

beach resolves itself into a unity of form, its summer lagoons, its slopes and uplands merging; against the western sky and the falling bow of sun rise the silent and superb undulations of the dunes.

My nights are at their darkest when a dense fog streams in from the sea under a black, unbroken floor of cloud. Such nights are rare, but are most to be expected when fog gathers off the coast in early summer; this last Wednesday night was the darkest I have known. Between ten o'clock and two in the morning three vessels stranded on the outer beach—a fisherman, a four-masted schooner, and a beam trawler. The fisherman and the schooner have been towed off, but the trawler, they say, is still ashore.

I went down to the beach that night just after ten o'clock. So utterly black, pitch dark, it was, and so thick with moisture and trailing showers, that there was no sign whatever of the beam of Nauset; the sea was only a sound, and when I reached the edge of the surf the dunes themselves had disappeared behind. I stood as isolate in that immensity of rain and night as I might have stood in interplanetary space. The sea was troubled and noisy, and when I opened the darkness with an outlined cone of light from my electric torch I saw that the waves were washing up green coils of sea grass, all coldly wet and bright in the motionless and unnatural radiance. Far off a single ship was groaning its way along the shoals. The fog was compact of the finest moisture; passing by, it spun itself into my lens of light like a kind of strange, aërial, and liquid silk. Effin Chalke, the new coast guard, passed me going north, and told me that he had had news at the halfway house of the schooner at Cahoon's.

It was dark, pitch dark to my eye, yet complete darkness, I imagine, is exceedingly rare, perhaps unknown in outer nature. The nearest natural approximation to it is probably the gloom of forest country buried in night and cloud. Dark as the night was here, there was still light on the surface of the planet. Standing on the shelving beach, with the surf breaking at my feet, I could see the endless wild uprush, slide, and withdrawal of the sea's white rim of foam. The men at Nauset tell me that on such nights they follow along this vague crawl of whiteness, trusting to habit and a sixth sense to warn them of their approach to the halfway house.

Animals descend by starlight to the beach. North, beyond the dunes, muskrats forsake the cliff and nose about in the driftwood and weed, leaving intricate trails and figure eights to be obliterated by the day; the lesser folk—the mice, the occasional small sand-colored toads, the burrowing moles—keep to the upper beach and leave their tiny footprints under the overhanging wall. In autumn skunks, beset by a shrinking larder, go beachcombing early in the night. The animal is by preference a clean feeder and turns up his nose at rankness. I almost stepped on a big fellow one night as I was walking north to meet the first man south from Nauset. There was a scamper, and the creature ran up the beach from under my feet; alarmed he certainly was, yet was he contained and continent. Deer are frequently seen, especially north of the light. I find their tracks upon the summer dunes.

Years ago, while camping on this beach north of Nauset, I went for a stroll along the top of the cliff at break of dawn. Although the path followed close enough along the edge, the beach below was often hidden, and I looked directly from the height to the flush of sunrise at sea. Presently the path, turning, approached the brink of the earth precipice, and on the beach below, in the cool, wet rosiness of dawn, I saw three deer playing. They frolicked, rose on their hind legs, scampered off, and returned again, and were merry. Just before sunrise they trotted off north together down the beach toward a hollow in the cliff and the path that climbs it.

All night long the lights of coastwise vessels pass at sea, green lights going south, red lights moving north. Fishing schooners and flounder-draggers anchor two or three miles out, and keep a bright riding-light burning on the mast. I see them come to anchor at sundown, but I rarely see them go, for they are off at dawn. When busy at night, these fishermen illumine their decks with a scatter of oil flares. From shore, the ships might be thought afire. I have watched the scene through a night glass. I could see no smoke, only the waving flares, the reddish radiance on sail and rigging, an edge of reflection overside, and the enormous night and sea beyond.

One July night, as I returned at three o'clock from an expedition north, the whole night, in one strange, burning instant, turned into a phantom day. I stopped and, questioning, stared about. An enormous meteor, the largest I have ever seen, was consuming itself in an effulgence of light west of the zenith. Beach and dune and ocean appeared out of nothing, shadowless and motionless, a landscape whose every tremor and vibration were stilled, a landscape in a dream.

All winter long I slept on a couch in my larger room, but with the coming of warm weather I have put my bedroom in order— I used it as a kind of storage space during the cold season—and returned to my old and rather rusty iron cot. Every once in a while, however, moved by some obscure mood, I lift off the bedclothing and make up the couch again for a few nights. I like the seven windows of the larger room, and the sense one may have there of being almost out of doors. My couch stands alongside the two front windows, and from my pillow I can look out to sea and watch the passing lights, the stars rising over ocean, the swaying lanterns of the anchored fishermen, and the white spill of the surf whose long sound fills the quiet of the dunes.

Ever since my coming I have wanted to see a thunderstorm bear down upon this elemental coast. A thunderstorm is a "tempest" on the Cape. The quoted word, as Shakespeare used it, means lightning and thunder, and it is in this old and beauti-

ful Elizabethan sense that the word is used in Eastham. When a
schoolboy in the Orleans or the Wellfleet High reads the Shake-
spearean play, its title means to him exactly what it meant to
the man from Stratford; elsewhere in America, the term seems
to mean anything from a tornado to a blizzard. I imagine that
this old significance of the word is now to be found only in
certain parts of England and Cape Cod.

On the night of the June tempest, I was sleeping in my larger
room, the windows were open, and the first low roll of thunder
opened my eyes. It had been very still when I went to bed, but
now a wind from the west-nor'west was blowing through the
windows in a strong and steady current, and as I closed them
there was lightning to the west and far away. I looked at my
watch; it was just after one o'clock. Then came a time of waiting
in the darkness, long minutes broken by more thunder, and
intervals of quiet in which I heard a faintest sound of light surf
upon the beach. Suddenly the heavens cracked open in an immense instant of pinkish-violet lightning. My seven windows
filled with the violent, inhuman light, and I had a glimpse of the
great, solitary dunes staringly empty of familiar shadows; a tremendous crash then mingled with the withdrawal of the light,
and echoes of thunder rumbled away and grew faint in a returning rush of darkness. A moment after, rain began to fall gently
as if someone had just released its flow, a blessed sound on a roof
of wooden shingles, and one I have loved ever since I was a
child. From a gentle patter the sound of the rain grew swiftly
to a drumming roar, and with the rain came the chuckling of
water from the eaves. The tempest was crossing the Cape,
striking at the ancient land on its way to the heavens above
the sea.

Now came flash after stabbing flash amid a roaring of rain,
and heavy thunder that rolled on till its last echoes were swal-
lowed up in vast detonations which jarred the walls. Houses

were struck that night in Eastham village. My lonely world, full of lightning and rain, was strange to look upon. I do not share the usual fear of lightning, but that night there came over me, for the first and last time of all my solitary year, a sense of isolation and remoteness from my kind. I remember that I stood up, watching, in the middle of the room. On the great marshes the lightning surfaced the winding channels with a metallic splendor and arrest of motion, all very strange through windows blurred by rain. Under the violences of light the great dunes took on a kind of elemental passivity, the quiet of earth enchanted into stone, and as I watched them appear and plunge back into a darkness that had an intensity of its own I felt, as never before, a sense of the vast time, of the thousands of cyclic and uncounted years which had passed since these giants had risen from the dark ocean at their feet and given themselves to the wind and the bright day.

Fantastic things were visible at sea. Beaten down by the rain, and sheltered by the Cape itself from the river of west wind, the offshore brim of ocean remained unusually calm. The tide was about halfway up the beach, and rising, and long parallels of low waves, forming close inshore, were curling over and breaking placidly along the lonely, rain-drenched miles. The intense crackling flares and quiverings of the storm, moving out to sea, illumined every inch of the beach and the plain of the Atlantic, all save the hollow bellies of the little breakers, which were shielded from the light by their overcurling crests. The effect was dramatic and strangely beautiful, for what one saw was a bright ocean rimmed with parallel bands of blackest advancing darkness, each one melting back to light as the wave toppled down upon the beach in foam.

Stars came out after the storm, and when I woke again before sunrise I found the heavens and the earth rain-washed, cool, and clear. Saturn and the Scorpion were setting, but Jupiter

33

was riding the zenith and paling on his throne. The tide was low in the marsh channels; the gulls had scarcely stirred upon their gravel banks and bars. Suddenly, thus wandering about, I disturbed a song sparrow on her nest. She flew to the roof of my house, grasped the ridgepole, and turned about, apprehensive, inquiring . . . 'tsiped her monosyllable of alarm. Then back toward her nest she flew, alighted in a plum bush, and, reassured at last, trilled out a morning song.

[To Miss Coatsworth]

Oui je suis de retour from my Coast Guard trip. It was in many ways quite the most wonderful experience I've ever had on land. I spent two weeks with them, living at the stations, and going out on patrol every night either at midnight or two-thirty— some eighty-five miles afoot through all kinds of weather. And what tales about warm stoves, wreckage coming ashore, voices and cries in the wild dark, and no ship to be seen, ships in a bitter northeast gale with sails frozen hard as boards and the dead men in the rigging mummies of ice, the terrible wreck of the Castagna, the death of the crew, and the shivering, half-alive canary found next morning in the soppy cabin, the sandstorms of Peaked Hill, the long lonely patrols between the vague white confusion of the surf and that fearful, frozen, unclimbable 120-foot bank—it was all elemental, splendid, life at melodrama pitch. I went six miles through the worst storm, guided only by the surf thundering at our feet, the world seemed to swallow one up; one seemed to sink into a kind of interplanetary gulf. And oh have you seen Monomoy Point? A long sand spit, twelve miles long and a mile wide, the end of it a shifting shoal of sand filled with horrible sunken lagoons full of seepage black as watery tar, dead grass lying flat in the marsh, utter loneliness, and moldering wrecks rotting in the mires. A House of Usher

*country. Never saw anything like it. And from the watchtower
one sees the sunken shoals, huge covered islands, mottles of
yallerish water with fierce blue-black channels running between
'em—channels in which the opposing tides meet and kick up
pyramids of water like the bases of a waterspout.*

*I went patrolling there in a wild rainstorm that died away into
a fog. You would have laughed to see me in my costume. I wore
an old blue suit, husky shoes, socks pulled up outside my trousers,
my Navy knitted cap, my Navy blue jacket, and my French army
belt buckled on outside. I carried my change of things in a
rucksack on my back. When I could get a lift from station to
station I took it, but often I had to walk six miles along that
elemental beach from one place to the other. You wouldn't see
a house or another person all the six miles. But it was great fun
swinging along with my pack, and the utter loneliness was part of
the experience.*

[From "The Year at High Tide"]

The winter sea was a mirror in a cold, half-lighted room, the
summer sea is a mirror in a room burning with light. So abun-
dant is the light and so huge the mirror that the whole of a
summer day floats reflected on the glass. Colors gather there,
sunrise and twilight, cloud shadows and cloud reflections, the
pewter dullness of gathering rain, the blue, burning splendor of
space swept free of every cloud. Light transfixes ocean, and some
warmth steals in with the light, but the waves that glint in the
sun are still a tingling cold.

On Monday morning last, as I sat writing at my west windows,
I heard a tern give a strange cry, and on looking out and up I
saw a bird harrying the female marsh hawk, of whose visits to

35

the dunes I have already told. The sea bird's battle cry was entirely new to my ear. *"Ke'ke'ke'aow!"* he cried; there was warning in the harsh, horny cry, danger and anger. The greater bird, flapping her wings as if they were spreads of paper—the winging of this hawk, near earth, is sometimes curiously like the winging of a butterfly—made no answer, but sank to earth slowly, wings outspread for a long half minute on the shell-strewn floor of the sandpit forty feet back from my house. Thus perched motionless, she might have been a willing mark. Scolding without pause, the tern, who had followed the enemy down into the pit, then rose and dived on her as he might have dived on a fish. The hawk continued to sit motionless. It was an extraordinary scene. Regaining level wing just above the hawk's head, the tern instantly climbed and dived again. At his third dive, the hawk took off, flying ahead and low across the sandpit. The battle then moved into the dunes, and the last I saw of the affair was the hawk abandoning the hills and flying south unpursued far out over the marsh.

Watching the hawk thus a-squat on the sand in a summer intensity of light, with the grey sea bird angrily assailing her, there came into my mind a thought of the ancient Egyptian representations of animals and birds. For this hawk in the pit was the Horus Hawk of the Egyptians, the same poise, the same dark blood-fierceness, the same authority. The longer I live here and the more I see of birds and animals, the greater my admiration becomes for those artists who worked in Egypt so many long thousand years ago, drawing, painting, carving in the stifling quiet of the royal tombs, putting here ducks frightened out of the Nile marshes, here cattle being herded down a village street, here the great sun vulture, the jackal, and the snake. To my mind, no representations of animals equal these Egyptian renderings. I do not write in praise of faithful delineation or pictorial usage—though the Egyptian drew from his model with

36

care—but of the unique power to reach, understand, and portray the very psyche of animals. The power is particularly notable in Egyptian representations of birds. A hawk of stone carved in hardest granite on a temple wall will have the soul of all hawks in his eyes. Moreover, there is nothing human about these Egyptian creatures. They are self-contained and aloof as becomes folk of a first and intenser world.

[Notebook from Eastham village, late summer]

Home by the moors again at sundown—every bit of it moving and beautiful, one light on the moors, a deserted house, fringe of locust tree against the sunset, its change of quality against the light and towards it.

Truro church superb at nightfall. The evening stars over the dune edge, monstrous dark of the bay side.

Arrived at Eastham about 7:45, then a step outdoors to see the beloved sight of Orion rising from the sea, to see the "great stars aslant" for the first time of the year. Always for me a moving event. The moon was towards its full, the night still, and I could hear the crash of the separate breakers from the dunes. The stars were south of the Fo'castle—his belt still hidden in the clouds, his feet in the far surges of the sea.

[From "Orion Rises on the Dunes"]

The economy of nature, its checks and balances, its measurements of competing life—all this is its great marvel and has an ethic of its own.

37

A human life, so often likened to a spectacle upon a stage, is more justly a ritual. The ancient values of dignity, beauty and poetry which sustain it are of nature's inspiration; they are born of the mystery and beauty of the world. Do no dishonor to the earth lest you dishonor the spirit of man. Hold your hands out over the earth as over a flame. To all who love her, who open to her the doors of their veins, she gives of her strength, sustaining them with her own measureless tremor of dark life. Touch the earth, love the earth, honor the earth, her plains, her valleys, her hills and her seas; rest your spirit in her solitary places. For the gifts of life are the earth's and they are given to all, and they are the songs of birds at daybreak, Orion and the Bear, and dawn seen over ocean from the beach.

IN MAINE

Chimney Farm and the Herb Attic

From the beginning Henry was happy at Chimney Farm. For a study he most often used the big herb attic with its two small windows and its big dormer. Under the slant of the roof he had bookcases built, and installed a wood stove and a bed where he slept sometimes on stormy nights, so that he might hear the rain directly over his head.

It may have been in this room, used largely when the children were at camp or boarding school and the house was quiet, that he began to think about herbs in connection with a garden. He had named it the herb attic on our first coming to the farm because of the dried herbs we found still hanging there.

At first we spent only six months of the year at the farm, returning off-season for a week at a time, learning how much work goes into making a house comfortable when one depends on oil lamps, wood stoves and the cistern pump.

But changes came. After the first few years we had electricity and hot water and a furnace. We had many friends with whom we went for tea or cocktails, but more often we sat talking of old times in the kitchens of our farm neighbors. In summer we swam and paddled the canoe we had brought back from Old Town. In fall, we took to the wide acres of woodland, clearing out old wood-roads and cutting narrow paths to our favorite heights and coves. In winter we explored on snowshoes.

He published small pieces. I have said Henry could write deeply only of what he had experienced deeply: the beauty and wonder of the year circling over the Fo'castle and its solitary Outermost Householder; the rural year on the rather remote farm in Maine with its fields and woods sloping down to Damariscotta Pond; the herb garden he had fostered there; the St. Lawrence which he had followed from Lake Ontario to the sea and seen in all lights and at all times of the year. These were part of him and to these he could give his best.

For the rest, he did a few books of small importance but mostly he followed the farm routine that he loved, living here in his chosen state and house until his death in 1968, less than two months short of his eightieth birthday.

WHITE PINE AND BLUE WATER

[From the Introduction]

The State of Maine, unlike the New England lying to the south
and west, has its roots in the eighteenth century rather than in
the seventeenth. Although the region was known and settlements
had been made since the early days of the North Atlantic
fisheries, it was not till after the fall of Quebec and the surrender
of French Canada that the province could be regarded as safely
ready for plantation. Those interested in the quality of Maine
will find it important to note that being of the eighteenth century, the state had no background of seventeenth-century Massachusetts Calvinism, which the passing years had modified to
something less fanatical and grim. Maine was never Puritan, in
the historical and theological sense of that unyielding term. The
earliest settlements had been Anglican, an influence still vigorous
in the life of the state; the present mood is evangelical.

Not till the second great struggle of the age, the American
Revolution, had been won did pioneers arrive in numbers,
following with their oxen a primitive coast road already blazed
or disembarking from some small vessel which had made the
run "downeast" from the ports of Massachusetts. (The term
"downeast" is a sailors' phrase for the country to which the

43

course from Massachusetts lay "down" the prevailing southwest wind of summer; the "east" has reference to the fact that the Maine coast lay about due northeast magnetic from Boston in the later eighteenth century. As there is an annual variation, the magnetic course has since altered.) What lay ahead was New England's contemporary frontier, and on they came, the adventurous and the hardy, the seafarers and the people of the barn and plough, following that North Star which was later, and with such wise insight, made to figure on the state shield. A wilderness paradise both awaited and confronted them. The "province of Maine" had remained as nature had made it, clothed in the green of the ancient forest, and, in its being, unsullied and remote. The woods teemed with game, the rivers, ponds, and coastal waters were aswarm with fish, and the great pines stood massed and untroubled in the wilderness.

On they came, and defending itself against the arrival of man, the earth put on its armor of snow and sometimes arctic cold. To use a favorite word of the Maine vocabulary, its prizes were to be for the "rugged"; from the first it would have no headlong frontier scramble, disorderly and squalid; it demanded courage, character, and endurance. To this day, the state grants its people the inestimable boon—inestimable in twentieth-century America —of not having things both passive and too easy. It makes demands.

Those who would understand the particular quality of Maine must first, perhaps, take thought of this element of the frontier. For the frontier is still a part of our lives. Beyond the coast and the farming country opening inland along the rivers lies the great north woodland, thousands of square miles of it, flowing earthwise across the mountains to the political frontier of Canada —with the noble fortress of Katahdin at its heart. A moose may take it into its head to cross U.S. Route 1, but there is no pressure of the tragic, crowded, and inescapable mass to confuse and smother one about; one does not have to elbow or gasp to remain an individual and a human being. Modern mass pressures, too, of their very selves, mean a compulsion towards a nonhuman specialization, and this the State-of-Mainer has happily avoided; in the old American tradition, he can still do many things and do them well. An element which is perhaps a social inheritance of the kind of pioneering which did occur is the goodwill and the neighborliness of a Maine community.

The other pillar of the state is certainly the presence of the sea. The North Atlantic brings to the coast, and, indeed, to the entire region, another aspect of physical and spiritual freedom and enlargement. Let it be remembered that no coastal people is ever provincial.

I cannot close without remarking that Maine enjoys being Maine. Something of the eighteenth-century gusto of living continues here, and there is a positive enjoyment of adventure, character, and circumstance. Bulwarked by the tradition of an ancestral New England, by the discipline of the wilderness and the ordinances of the sea, the way of life has faced the age of the machine and preserved its communal goodwill and the human values. Here one still thinks of life as life and not as existence.

[To his wife, on his first sight
of the farm in winter 1931]

Jake Day and I have had an afternoon of outdoor adventure.
We faced a five-mile walk over a side road scarcely broken out, a
road climbing and descending two great hills from whose

45

summits one could look over a great Maine wilderness wood
to the Camden Mountains blue and white in the far air. Deep
snow everywhere, five feet of it on the fields, and roadside
drifts as high as my head, heavy, water-cemented snow—snow
and space and woods. At the end of it a farm, an old, old couple
with cheery blue eyes, a deep well in living rock, a grandfather's
clock, and a library of paper novels of the 1880–90 "Can you
forget her?" kind. Then across a most beautiful pine and beech
and hemlock pasture to a slope in deep pines and hemlocks,
then a cove, a dream of a cove, woods all around, no cottages,
nothing but superb trees—"old growth" as they say here—an
amphitheater of snow and towering green, the bush beneath
buried deep save for some out-struggled twig here and there; the
floor of the cove, an untrodden, stainless carpet of level snow.
(I had been fitted to borrowed snowshoes at the farm and was
carrying-on perfectly easily and liking every step. My very
worldly Piccadilly blue overcoat plus snowshoes was voted a
great success.) Across the cove sky, a passing, very high, of
maenad clouds.

[To his wife, on his first night at
Chimney Farm, summer 1931]

So the afternoon storm, black as pitch, broken and bright with
sharp lightning, and roaring long with a tropical rain, came to an
end in brooding vapor touched with gold and the presence, but
not the appearance, of the western sun; and the men went home,
leaving the house empty of voices, and Henry, with more of a
sigh than a leap of the heart, prepared to spend his first night
in the house. First he went over to the Rollinses'—oh, nicest
and best of Philemons and Baucises!—and found the grey

kitchen brisk and cheery with the end of the storm and the
western gold, and genial with the smell of supper in the oven,
and there did buy a quart of golden milk which brought back to
his tongue the remembered taste of country milk on a small
boy's tongue long ago, the taste milk had before cows grew so
scientific, then half a dozen eggs, and a present of tomatoes.
Home then to the house, now quieter, as if the stir of men's
voices and their moving about were a thing which left in one
first great ebb then forsook the corners, now darker as the
thunderstorm, empty of its thunder, gathered greyly. Supper,
then, in the "buttery" then round and abouts the house with a
lamp, and so on upstairs to the room overlooking the lake. The
house very, very still. On the chair, old work clothes; in the bed
propped up, myself; and on the table, my clock, my knife with
its Japanese cord, and faced towards me, my picture of you and
Meg.

[To his wife, several months later]

I am writing in the kitchen (which like all good farm kitchens
is also a living room). Walking round a moment ago to look at
your grape arbor again and consider what might be done with it,
I heard across the lovely, wet, sunlit autumn countryside the
rumble of a farm-cart's wheel and the fine challenge of a cock,
and hearing them I thought of how all these earthy things carry
me back to France, back to Ste. Catherine-sous-Rivière, the
village in the Monts Lyonnais where I lived quite a fair share
of my French year. The mountains were about twenty miles in
from the Rhône, one side running parallel to the river, another
facing south on the wide plain of an ancient side-valley tributary
to the Rhône. I used to take a little train across the foothill

47

country lying west of Lyons, get off at the end of the line at
Mormant, a village-town at the foot of the massif (for it was a
"massif" rather than a range) and then continue to Ste.
Catherine on foot. The climbing road, some ten kilometers
altogether, went first up the Rhône-wards slope, then turned a
steep grassy descent—almost a sort of grassy precipice—and then
emerged on the southern flank, high, high above the wide
valley and its scatter of red-roofed village huddles with the
usual outlying few farms. Thirty or forty kilometers across was
the superb solitary mountain, Mont Pilat of the Cévennes, a
glorious mountain which in winter across the "brume" of the
morning hillside, rose distant and violet and chasmed with pure
radiations of new snow. Ste. Catherine, if I forget the farm
boardinghouses Mother and I were sent to in the summer, was
the first place in which I encountered and knew and loved the
earth. I hadn't had any true chance before. We had a cottage
on Quincy bay but Nature, as well as the very decent
"comfortably-offs"—in the Quincy valuations—was in a suburban
mood there; she went yachting in a catboat on Saturday
afternoons and arranged her tides as if they had to take trains.
There was no poetry. Fugitive glimpses, perhaps, but no deep,
underlying mood. Then came France, and the earth and the
revelation of the earth.

The stones in our little Maine burial plot are being revealed
by autumn, the twin trees are glories of russet gold. Their leaves
are falling this morning like things dropped from a lady's hand.

HERBS AND THE EARTH

[From "Of Herbs and the Earth"]

It was a pleasant fancy of the ancients that the lights of heaven, the sun and the moon, the errant planets and the military and ordered stars sang each his song as they moved in harmony upon their paths, ennobling thus the shell of space with music. Were mortal ears prepared to sustain such melodies, it was thought, one might chance to hear, at cloudless noon, in a high and quiet land, a sound of the great cry of the sun, and by night and the moon another music not of earth brushing against earth and the blood. In this celestial harmony what song, then, sang the earth? What vast and solemn music did this our planet make as turning upon its poles it wheeled through the universal void rolling up its cities to the sun and its fields down to the night? Was the sound but the unconfused and primal voice of the planet welling forever from its cores of stone, or did a sound of rivers and many oceans, of leaves and immeasurable rain mingle to make a mysterious harmony? And might a listening god, perhaps, have heard echoes of man, the shrilling of a plough turned from earth into earth and stones, or a woman singing her dream and her content?

It is only when we are aware of the earth and of the earth as poetry that we truly live. Ages and people which sever the earth from the poetic spirit, or do not care, or stop their ears with knowledge as with dust, find their veins grown hollow and their hearts an emptiness echoing to questioning.

Here in this pleasant arbor by the herbs, with the grape over-head, and Basil in flower in the open sun, here in this quiet varied with an early summer sound of country birds, one may well muse awhile on how the soul may possess and keep her earth inheritance. The age in which we live is curious and be-wildered; it is without a truly human past and may be without a human future, and so abruptly it came that one might imagine some cosmic spirit or wayward daimon to have reached down of a moment and plucked man by the hair. It has lost the earth, but found (since the comfortable century of philosophers in dressing gowns) a something which it calls "nature," and of which it speaks with enthusiasm and embalms in photographs. It has lost as well the historic sense, the poignant and poetic recognition of the long continuity of man, that sense within our hearts which is moved by a chance print in an old book of a countryman ploughing with oxen beside ruins overgrown with Fennel while to one side women clap cymbals together to calm the swarming bees.

A garden of herbs need be no longer than the shadow of a bush, yet within it, as in no other, a mood of the earth ap-proaches and encounters the spirit of man. Beneath these ances-tral leaves, these immemorial attendants of man, these servants of his magic and healers of his pain, the earth underfoot is the earth of poetry and the human spirit; in this small sun and shade flourishes a whole tradition of mankind. This flower is Athens; this tendril, Rome; a monk of the Dark Ages tended this green against the wall; with this scented leaf were kings welcomed in the morning of the world. Lovely and timeless, rooted at once in gardens and in life, the great herbs come to the gardener's hand our most noble heritage of green.

It is the very early morning, the house is not yet awake, and in the garden refreshed with night the bees are working in the herbs. The frailer spikes of Hyssop sway under their weight, bending over like birches swung by boys; the Marjoram shakes and nods to their fumbling and climbing and alighting; on the spikes of Basil they thrust their whole heads into the larger flowers and drive off newcomers with a buzz. Herbs bring bees, bees with their immortal air of fable and the golden age. Labiate flowers please them, for the honeyed reward is generous and kept sheltered for their taking.

Now sweeps a high wind over the farming land, shaking like a banner the fields which today await the mower, rushing wayward this way and that through the fruiting grass, all in a long lashing sound of wind and leaves. The sparrows who have come to glean in yesterday's greener stubble hold close to the earth, their brownish groups fly low, but the higher swallows are caught by the wind and soaring are blown about; the processional clouds move white. What winds shall blow, fall what lustral rains that the ancient sense of the beauty and integrity of the earth shall presently reawaken in the indifferent blood? Or must some great and furious storm (and such storms come) sweep clear the whole coast of the soul of man and restore him thus to his humanity? For man is of a quickening spirit and the earth, the strong, incoming tides and rhythms of nature move in his blood and being; he is an emanation of that journeying god the sun, born anew in the pale south and the hollow winter, the slow murmur and the long crying of the seas are in his veins, the influences of the moon, and the sound of rain beginning. Torn from earth and unaware, without the beauty and the terror, the mystery and ecstasy so rightfully his, man is a vagrant in space, desperate for the inhuman meaninglessness which has opened about him, and with his every step becoming something less than man.

Peace with the earth is the first peace. Unto so great a mystery, to paraphrase a noble saying, no one path leads, but many paths. What pleasant paths begin in gardens, leading beside the other great mystery of nature, the mystery of the growing green thing with its mute passion and green will. The day's high wind is walled off from the herbs, only the taller leaves stirring a little in the fringes of the gusts, the sun mounts from the southeast into the south, the black-and-yellow bees continue their timeless song. Beautiful and ancient presences of green, dear to man and the human spirit, let us walk awhile beside your leaves.

[From "Of Ten Great Herbs"]

We have had three weeks, almost a month, of rainless August heat. Last night, soon after the lamps were lit, I saw the first small drops on the outer darkness of the panes, and presently from under the kitchen floor the faint whisper of water trickling into the cistern could be heard in the silence of the room. This morning, the whole landscape is renewed, and the garden has its own good smell again of rain-wet earth and leaves. The green life of earth is a deeper life than we know, having its roots in touch with the waters under the earth, with those rills flowing unseen out of ledges deep in the ground. It is when the garden is unable to drink its fill from beneath, when the living ascent of moisture from the deeper earth to root earth is impeded, that plants begin to take on that lifeless air and curious, lifeless feel which surface water never quite dispels. In the court a woodpecker flies into the apple tree, making his way through the leaves without a sound; trees, sky, grass, house, herb garden, and flowers all shine together in a sun with a peaceful air, and walking out to see, I notice that the fine-leaved plants are still comfortably drenched whilst those with simpler and entire leaves are already dry.

Whenever I walk among the herbs at noon, at that hour when

a Spanish country saying will have it that the forces of the earth
are at their exaltation of power, I can never pass one of the great
Basils in the sun without a thought beginning there of the fantastic wonder of the whole green life of earth. Pivoted upon its
share of soil, potent with its intensity of living, symmetrical and
predetermined to symmetry, a fine plant of Basil is a form, a
gathering together of that mysterious vitality of green whose
veins draw up the earth itself, and whose impulse of life is the
other side of that rhythm of life stirring with us in our blood.
What a passion for life plants reveal, what a body and desire
of life dwell in the dark of roots and the hunger under the
earth! What will they not endure to live and bear, not surmount,
of caprice and outrage, of attack and disaster, if they can but lift
one flower from the ruin. What a sense of will there is in the
vine, in the groping of the tendril, in the ultimate seizure and
adherence! Denied the animal resource of flight, an intensity of
life is their ark and weapon; fixed upon earth they can but fight
death with life. We are not conscious enough in our human
world of this other shaping of life beside us, taking little account
of its presence and its ways, yet without such an awareness our
thought of life must remain a thing of our own firesides where
none see beyond the flame.

In making their gardens and choosing their flowers, the ancients
had a profound feeling for the lovely quality of fragrance. Mile
upon mile beyond Augustan Rome lay the rose gardens which
provided the city with its favorite flower; the Dark Ages saved
for us the herbs, keeping alive in their vast and unpeopled ruin
such plants as Spearmint and Parsley, which are so human and
old that they are not to be found in nature; the Elizabethan
flower and herb lists were an old-fashioned floral vase of pleasant
smells. For fragrance is indeed what the past well knew it to be, a

53

refreshment and a strength, a sweet and human pleasure, an exorciser of demons from the body and the besieged and troubled spirit. Subtlest of influences, touching the emotion directly, asking nothing from the mind, it not only wakes in us an emotion of place, but summons up as well a poignant emotion of ourselves as we were in time and the place remembered. The odor of a ploughed field in the spring is like a hand laid upon the heart, having in it all the beauty, the poignancy, and the tenderness of earthly living, all the poetry of the melancholy and ecstasy of spring, of the branch, the new leaf and the warm wind, and the sinking of some last great and solitary winter star.

This noontime, while the men were resting from the mowing, I saw something very curious happen in the field. The hay had been cut upon our upper slopes and lay drying in the stubble, and further down where the grass had been cut a day before, stood a haycock loosely piled. Suddenly between me and the glimpse of the team unharnessed and our neighbors eating dinner in the shade came a small and local whirlwind which crossed the road like a presence, and began its journey down the slope, picking up the hay. The air in its path was presently a wild shower of new hay tossed fifty and sixty feet high, more flying up as the vortex grew in its motion down the hill. It then took the top from the pile, scattered it over the field, and swept on across the uncut lower slope to the lake, darkened it with a cat's-paw path and vanished like a djinn from a bottle halfway to the other side. Straws and tousles of hay drifted down from the sky, lodging in the leaves of the apple trees and strewing all the nearer road, and presently all was as it had been or nearly so, and the farm bell rang for the noonday meal.

Save for the djinn which lately troubled the field, a true country peace hangs in the hot sunlit air, and from the garden I follow with my ear the rattling click of the mowing machine to the end of its swale, hearing then the shout and Ho! to the horses and the sound again beginning.

Here in the North, summer comes earlier to its close, and the sign of the turn of the year is less a first thinning and coloring of leaves than a first great drenching rain. Beginning at night, the small crepitation of the rain wakes the sleeper in the attic chamber, who listens awhile for joy of the sound and is again asleep, the grey morning is confused with rain, and all day long the wind flattens against the house, blowing across the lake from the east and the distant sea. When the weather breaks and the sun again shines, it is autumn. The trees are still in apparent summer leaf, but the substance of the leaves is dry for all the storming, and enough have been blown down to reveal a gleam of the lake through green which was once a wall. It is the lovelier, brighter light of autumn which gilds this seeming summer, the lake is a brighter blue, and a new quiet has come upon the land.

Of what plant it was which first became an ally of man, who shall speak with authority? Was it the wheat with its sacred spear or barley of the dry and fruitful whisper or a wildling perhaps tried for a season and returned again to companions of the grass? One by one, now taken from the wood, now from the river mire, now seized from the barrens and the stone, the plants came into human life, and among the first were the herbs. Was the earliest to come perhaps a magical thing, some potency of earth mysteriously united with powers regnant in nature but not yet become as gods? There grows in the garden here a very ancient plant which has been a part of the magic and religion of the most diverse European cultures, in England being a sacred plant of the Druids, in Scandinavia a plant of the priests of Thor, in Greece and Rome a plant so holy that no other might be used to brush the altars of Olympian Jove. Yet it is not a stately plant but a quite simple one, almost a thing of the roadsides and the fields. "Hierobotane" the Greeks called it, the "holy plant"; and "herba sacra" the Romans. To us it is Spike or Herbal Vervain, the *Verbena officinalis* of Linnaeus.

To those interested in magic and religion, there is no herb in the garden more worthy of attention, for this simple plant without fragrance, without an outer look of power, without a flower of significance, was singled out from among all other plants and herbs as the most sacred of the growing things of earth between the Pillars of Hercules and the roots of the Caucasus.

[From "Of Many Herbs of Many Kinds"]

It is winter, and the short-lived and silent day has come to an end over the great landscape of snow, closing at sundown with a sky of frozen pink and channels of clearest green; now clouds and the night make together a greater silence and dark; and snow has again begun to fall. Within the house the lamps are lit, each filled to its brim with oil against the long usage of the hours, and the little parlor is comfortable with yellow light and a wood stove's fragrant warmth. It is yellow birch which burns in that sable bastille, yellow birch which kindles so readily and whose bright flames send up from chimneys so unmistakable a smoke. And still it snows, falling through the pitch-black and windless night, feathering over the uneven footing of the shoveled paths, ridging twig and branch anew, and deepening the white levels of the lake.

Where the great Basils stood, and the Lavender was put to have its share of the sun, is now all under a good three feet of snow. No longer the wild, beautiful cries of the loon break at strange hours from the lake, on unsettled, rainy days prophesying still more rain; the crows are with us only when it thaws. Jays are now the most familiar birds, coming to the doors of barns for seeds of fodder which have been shaken from the lofts down upon the snow, and taking to the fence like sparrows when the farm cats pass. The partridges, too, are foraging. There are lilacs by the shed, and late yesterday afternoon, almost at nightfall, as I chanced to pass the huge, frozen bushes on my way to the spring, six of the birds broke from them in a commotion of winged sound, and vanished as by magic into the last of sunset and the luminous darkness on the fields.

A winter evening is the best of times to muse on plans for a garden, for, like Bunyan's *Pilgrim's Progress*, gardening is then carried on "under the similitude of a dream." The things we mean to have stand as we mean to have them, thrifty, beautiful, and a pretty tribute to our skill as gardeners; the things we have had, successes and less-than-successes, are something to go on from, are a part of garden history and our lives. On the table, tumbled over the books, on the floor beside the chair, are an armful of the herb-garden plans, catalogues, letters, leftovers, seed packets, garden notes, and general ambitions, and the aromatic scent of herb seeds is already in the lamplit air. Here in this corner, cut from a yellow envelope and sealed with a fold, is more of the Marjoram which is the Hyssop of Scripture, a green papery seed with a dry, agreeable, and delicately bitter smell—the Hyssop of the lintels of Egypt, and of that tragic draught offered and refused. Here is Coriander, rattling like dry rain in its small box, its seeds like chaffy pills, ancient Coriander of the delta of Egypt, first tasted long ago in a child's cake bought at a shop kept by an elderly Bavarian; here is Dill, fresh and pungent; Burnet which comes so readily from the earth; and the flat Angelica seed which tastes of juniper and bites the

57

tongue. But now to garden musings of the winter kind, and a talk of herbs while the fire blazes and the night is young.

[From "Epilogue in Spring"]

The earth emerges from the snow, lifting to the reassurance of the longer day her fields that have been as iron northward to the Pole, a new green lies in the dappled warmth upon the hill, and the winter-barren trees are great with spring. All day long, blown by a new and warmer wind, loose ice and sailing floes from the ice remaining on the lake have come tinkling like hollow glass into the shallows of the coves, there to drift glinting out of the light into the shadowy green of pines once more reflected on quiet water, there to strand and disappear. The waters under the earth and the waters upon it are everywhere unsealing, flowing from the new green of moss down the slope of ledges in the sun and gathering in clearest pools where the snow has melted in the woods. Crows pass between the spring sky and the dead grass touched with green, a new odor of water and open earth is in the wind, a door of the house stands open, and from a chimney-top a wreath of smoke falls off and mingles with the sky.

In the garden of the herbs, where the drifts stood so high, blown up the fenceless slope and against the house from the northeast, the brighter sun stands warm. Beneath their autumn covering of leaves and hemlock boughs remaining green, the mother roots stir in the earth, coming to life in that darkness where, as George Herbert said, they "keep house alone." Intricacy of leaf unborn, color drawn upwards out of the earth, fragrance and potency and beauty are here in secret being, soon to be manifest to the several senses, and at their roots a gift of the gardener's peace which none shall have who have not a deep peace with the earth, though the road to her seem but a path.

For beside that path lie the seasons and the ritual of the year, the vast adventures and journeyings of the sun, the towering of a wave to its breaking, the faithful wheeling of the moon, the sound of rain when there are no more leaves, and the furrow lengthening under the tug of hooves on a morning in spring. Sustained and molded of its immeasurable forces, it is by this mystery we exist, and by its poetic power in our lives that we attain the stature of human beings, having the sun to our right hand and the earth and the seas beneath us; without it becoming like the ghosts in Homer, houseless, and thin and dead, and crowding and whispering angrily for blood.

The quiet of winter is wearing through upon the land. Human voices which seemed lost in the vast of snow have again the open earth beneath them, and over the unfrozen soil, across field and pasture and darker wood comes the bold and distant cry of chanticleer. What a fine sound it is, that triple and unearthly cry, heard here in the garden through the pale quiet of the northern spring. All the animal defiance of circumstance and fate, all the acceptance and challenge of the animal blood come with it into our human world seeking an echo there, before melting away into the light. Pressing on with the sun the furrow shall follow north the sun retreating, and the earth shall be sown again and shall part, giving life to the seed and to the herbs of man's remembrance, the ancient leaves dear at once to plough- man and woman of the distaff, to priest and golden-circleted king.

[*To the Reverend Dr. J. Luther Neff*]

All goes well at home, goes as it does everywhere in America.
Things taking a somewhat familiar course on a ground uneasy
with the general apprehension. Anyway, people are better than
they were in 1929. That mad, half-parasitic, mammon-ish
jamboree, with its horrible self-satisfaction and poor old Cal
patting it on the back and saying that riches and money and
radios were ours because we were holy, and poor Hoover telling
us that radios and electric stoves were an end in themselves.
People now are beginning to question, and questioning is
growth. There was no growth possible before.

"The Outermost House" comes out this winter in a completely
new edition, pretty good for full Depression times. The general
impression roundabout is that things are somewhat better. But I
see no future for this form of civilization with its brutal egotism,
its absence of poetic relation to the earth, and its failure to give
the meagerest life religious significance.

[*To David McCord*]

For the last few days a large-ish flock of grackles has been
camping at the farm, and early this morning as I sat writing here
in my little "studio" in the field (damn it! why didn't I say
"study," as the other word has an intellectual climate of the 90's
cum 1900's and is grown musty)—but, to resume, the grackle
army came walking out all around me through the hayfield
stubble, and they are formidable walkers, exchanging gallantly,
left and right, the positions of their tall, mechanic legs; the sun
turning all their heads and capes to a beautiful peacock blue,
from which shone, full of avian vitality but devoid of expression
in any human term, a very busy bright lemon-yellow eye. I never

realized the creatures were so handsome. Later in the afternoon
they all flew down the sloping fields to the water, perching on a
lakeside elm bare of leaves, and making it look like an explorer's
photograph from some tropical region—"jub-jub birds roosting
at night"—you know, that sort of thing—all naked branches and
a multitude of bird-shaped lumps with a reflected sunset
"obbligato."

Good news. The herb book went yesterday to a second
printing. Betsy's new book, a charming tale of Colonial Virginia,
is out, "The Golden Horseshoe." We have bought a new kitchen
stove on the strength of it all, and when it is "set up," Betsy shall
light the first fire, for in the old magic the first fire on a new
hearth must always be lit by the woman of the house. It is not
necessary, but it is wise, continues the old tradition of wonder,
to lay the new fire on a few ashes or wood-coals from an old
hearth, best of all from one which has had humanity and
fulfillment about it, and at whose flames friends have warmed
their hands. And this we shall do.

I have been discussing with a correspondent "the mystical
experience," questioning now its reality, now affirming it, and
spreading before the mind the booby traps into which the
all-pervading flesh may lead the ecstatical unwary. My
correspondent tells of an incident reported by some student of
mysticism with a sense of humor—of a scholar who woke at night
with a quatrain ringing through his head, and an exaltation of
divine glory in his veins as if the quatrain held the secret of the
universe. He put it down, invisible flames and splendors guiding
his hand, and sank into a sleep of divine unconsciousness. In the
morning he woke to find he had written—

> Walker with one eye,
> Walker with two.
> Something to live for
> And nothing to do.

It is so perfect I suspect he really had melted into the divine mind!

[To F. Morton Smith, his brother-in-law]

We are back from Arizona and in Hingham, and it is snowing a perfectly horrible grey snow which has all the air of having been cut with nail scissors from a poorhouse rag. We are home but not yet at home, for though our bodies look sourly out on the trucks and Hingham harbor at low tide, our mental flesh is far away, striking Napoleon-at-ease attitudes on cow-ponies & getting ready to take the trail to the canyons. O! canyons of remembrance with your old, very old, rose-red walls, so beautifully lichened with a sort of emerald-verdigris, and you, O Salt River, flowing so unaccountably below, your hurrying stream a kind of naïve jade. And you, O Rimrock high in air, with your far, far away mountain walls turning at sundown one deep and even tender blue against the western light—the sky having taken on a new scale even as the earth; Rimrock with the Verde Valley below, all a wide mystery of little buttes and mesas, plains, sunken valley floors outlined by rushing brooks and already deeply green. And everywhere the sense of the American past, that past apart from tea and toast, family silver and portraits above the mantel, that other America of the waving corn and the corn meal in the bowl, the eagle's feather, and the sweet smell of pinyon smoke rising and darkening the limestone cliff.

In those divinest hours when we had the place to ourselves, I had, as I have had few times in life, the lovely joy of beauty and assured quiet. Schopenhauer says that the intellectual power of a mind is in parallel relation to its hatred of noise—a thing I've always found to be true. A noisy man is simply a noisy child and a noisy civilization is a child's civilization.

[In "The Contributors' Club," *Atlantic Monthly*]

Sound and Life

As I was once walking along a country road I heard to one side, across a field and through a screen of birches, the pleasant clang of hammer and anvil from a farmer's smithy, and pausing awhile in the rural quiet, I began to meditate on the history of sounds in human life, of how certain characteristic sounds had accompanied certain ages of history, and of how such sounds had vanished out of life, some, perhaps, to reappear, and others to be heard no more. Quickened by the neighboring clang, my mind imagined in its own ear a sound familiar to many centuries, the tapping of the armorer's hammer, and I wondered in what walled and old-fashioned city it had last been obscurely heard; and I thought, too, of the sound of arrows loosed by a great company of bowmen, and wondered in what heraldic battle the air had last filled with that arched and formidable humming.

In the beginning the world must have been very pleasantly still. The ancient quiet of earth, which is but a vulnerable fragment of the pure silence of space, had not yet gone to hide, like a spirit, in lonely places. Those vast, fantastic fragments that are the continents we know, each ringed with the timeless cadences and confusions of the sea, were full of that inland peace which begins where the ocean murmur dies away. The first sounds to visit human ears were those which are perhaps destined to be the last; that to which we listen, Adam heard. Spacing the quiet, men heard the lovely sounds of earth—rain in the deep woods on dying, late-summer leaves, the stir of trees at sunrise that have been still all night, the fiery snap of lightning, the song of a bird by a lake. A small and local sound of stone struck upon stone, that sharp, complete, integral click without vibration, must have been the first true "made" sound to part the ancient leaves, to be, for ages too vast for centuries to count, the tokening sound of man. Metal with its lengthening vibration then confused the stone, more voices jargoned (for this early world, it would seem, was filling up) the crowd din, and cries of archaic war arose, and presently beginning sounds of the arts and trades intruded with the numbered years.

So began the pageant, with the silences and sounds that have not died. For all our noises, the first quiet is nearer than we know. The inland stillness is a sea: if our sounds trouble it like fountains, like fountains they fall back and are no more; if it be gone to hide like a spirit, it can return like an armed man, and there were cities on the war front thus retaken. The voices of earth are likewise ours, harassed and lessened only in so far as they rise from the kingdom of creatures, but still oracles and gods. Secluded tribes still practice the arts of stone, and I have myself heard the attendant sound; there are yet people who make and use the primitive metal implements. For beginnings are often like the roots of trees, remaining below and unchanged in their nature, while there are change and development from them overhead.

What vanished sounds, what fine ghosts of the ear, rise from the known years! Screaming upon their axles, in a storm of dust and hoofs, the war chariots charge the Biblical plain; the measured plash of oars in banks rises from some galley bound for Ostia, the heavy wooden pound of the quartermaster's timing mace heard muffled from below decks; behind Pentelic colonnades, the stringed music of lost instruments mingles with a vast chanting before the gods. One hears the hiss of the snakes of Greek fire from Byzantine citadels; bells ringing against thunderstorms of Gothic cities; the popgun sound of Renaissance artillery; the rumble of the first coaches on the first good roads, and the howl of wind in the rigging of an eighteenth-century man-of-war in foul weather at anchor in the downs.

They are well gone; men will hear them no more; and in our own day the last sounds of the handicrafts descend, fighting gallantly, toward the same oblivion. It may be that they will hold their ultimate own, and presently mount, passing on their upward way the whole huge childishness of modern noise down-tumbling. What contemporary sound, one pauses to ask, will summon up our own strange years: The universal grind of gears when traffic starts again at a light, the demoniac tattoo of a riveter? In my own mind, it is something more subtle, more like the dry, merciless, electric tick one hears in the pressured silence of a power room, a small sound, obedient, without life, and astronomically alien to the bones of man.

There is one sound which catches the exact note of the nineteenth century—that era of rather simple machinery, growing populations, optimism, and more facts, which has now so largely collapsed, hammered by the war and disintegrated by the motor. It is the whistle of a locomotive at nightfall in the country. The sound is still the same piercing alarum it has always been; it has authority, its own self-confidence, and it is today almost elegiac and old-fashioned.

Perhaps there are far more old sounds alive than we know. All kinds of antique noises are still vigorous in that most conservative of all kingdoms, the sea, and in the country are a world of sounds so honorably old and so closely interwoven with the pattern of life that they are no more on the defensive than the wind in the trees. A few weeks ago, during haying time, I listened to the sounds rising from the fields, and marked them as the same I had heard in boyhood. From a wide swale under bordering trees rose the old, pleasant rattle of the mowing machine; I heard the clicking song of whetstone and scythe, the swish of some blade on the grindstone and the grindstone's treadle squeak; and late in the hot afternoon the grey, weathered rack passed us, fragrant and full-laden, creaking the same remembered creak, the same remembered groan.

Sound is more of life than we know. It is an inheritance and a thought, a mood and a power. Now inherent and determined, now create and mutable, it accompanies each life and age, resolved into one unperceived and enormous music. It is very much the earth's, being as much a part of landscape as the sky, even as the changing pitch of a brook along its course is part of the integrity of the moment in time and water. A whole way of life which has not given us one sweet and memorable sound can be justly suspect. Such a culture is only a kind of island in history, a weedy acre or two removed from the wide stream of the rhythm and tradition of man, doubtful soil in which the wise will note a proprietary print of cloven hoofs. The running stream will pass it, behind a bend and trees it will disappear, and Time will gather it into his illusion, and presently there will be ancient quiet again, and sounds born living of the spirit of man.

To a Lady Who Wrote "Wear Me Lightly"

Wear you lightly, love,
For all life I could not wear you so.
Heavily, then?
Oh, love, who feels the weight
Of his own heart?

> From the Japanese of Henrysan
> xxth century

Aquarius

There is a crust of snow upon these fields,
On the long fields descending to the lake,
Arching with granite of ice the running spring
And its delicate treble of speech below
    the armor of snow.
Breaking the arch, I wait till my pail
    overflows.

Only the wind has walked upon this hill,
Only the wind rippling the deserts of snow
Beneath his wayward and immortal feet.

67

Farm Breakfast

Cats with proud, heraldic tails
Borne like banners of a host,
Play about the floor awhile
As I turn to scan the toast,
And smile your small, archaic smile
Till the double saucer comes
Welcomed with a roll of drums.

To a Small Comic Dog

Pugs
Go with formal gardens
And with music-boxes
And with ladies in exquisite brocades
Reading Mr. Pope's Homer's Iliad
On an English summer afternoon
Near the artificial ruins.
The servants from Bombay bring sherbets
    and little cakes,
While from the corner of the conversation
    piece
The pug approves.

Oh, scampering and screw-tailed Scaramouche,
Lord of the level kingdoms of the floor,
How hold you so great store of gayety
Within the compass of so small a heart?

68

When You Leave Me

When you leave me,
It is as if a silence fell dead ripe upon
  the world.
There is no sound of brooks, no sound
Of any rill divided by a stone,
No more is heard
The faint, fluttering brush of any wing
In any wood surprised,
No wind on any hill, no cry
On the remotest shore,
Only the sound of the hours of the night
Passing me, awake, whispering
  your beloved name.

The Young Philosopher's Song

With a cat, with a bear
My morning's walk I share.
Paw in hand and claw in hand
Through the green midsummer land.

The listening birds within the wood
Approve our converse, sage and good,
And follow us among the trees
To overhear our homilies.

Till to the larger light of day
Forth from the wood we make our way
And well-contented homeward fare,
Cat, philosopher, and bear.

[Program note for a Farm and Home Week
banquet at the University of Maine]

The Great Realities

What has been taking place for the last hundred years is not
difficult to name. It is an alienation from Nature unexampled
in human history, and as it has gone its way, bringing both
comfort and violence, it has created a new kind of humanity
pitilessly ignorant alike of Nature and of human nature as well
as of the great earthly realities.

In all ages and in every nation, the farming population is the
force which has bound human beings to reality and the earth.
The farm, standing in its fields apart from the factory smoke
and the laboratories, is the living link with the mystery of
earthly existence, with the poetry and beauty of our human
heritage, with what may be possible and what impossible, with
life, with death. Without a farming population, a nation is never
healthy of spirit. It strays into the landscapes of illusion and
climbs the hill of dreams. Yet only through an awareness of
things as they are may we raise a humane and tolerant order.

Let us then share in the new hopes of men, but hold to the
ancient wisdoms of our agricultural heritage. The great verities
of our existence are not abrogated, the earth is still the earth,
the snow still the snow, night and day remain. Whatever comes
to pass, let us not forget that our world is the work of the
Divine Artificer, and that He looked upon His work and "saw
that it was good."

70

[*To his wife*]

*One of our possessions seems to be a fully equipped smithy with
a small hand forge, a pump and a trough and an iron pile—all
housed in an ancient shed. Jake and I, discovering it, looked at
it with interest and I wondered if there would ever come some
possible chance which would lead me to kindle a fire and strike
iron on the iron anvil mounted in turn upon a huge wood-block
of beech. Today, strolling round about one o'clock, I heard
voices and sounds from the smithy and discovered the two young
plumber's helpers out there shaping a bar of iron into such a
caulking tool as they wanted. One turned the little bellows fan,
the other did the striking, and the flames which came out of the
bed of soft coal were all like tall evergreens—a curious flame such
as I have never before seen.*

[*To David McCord*]

*It is ten below and a tiny, rain-like snow is falling from an arctic
monotony of pale, grey sky: you must pardon my calligraphy, for
my fingers are still benumbed after filling my wood baskets from
the wood-mountain in the covered shed. The two beer mugs
arrived from "the Artisans," and no other such present ever went
more to my heart. It has been my destiny to lead a rather solitary
life, I have chosen one wild place after another—but now that
the afternoon of life closes in east and west, I am sustained by
the thought of beloved and distinguished men of letters holding
a hand out to me across the snow. I should need the tongues of
men and angels to convey the joy the gifts gave me.*
    *We have had a typical regional tragedy close by us on the
coast. A fisherman and two grown boys went duck-hunting on a*

71

*wild day, and landed on a reef uncovered by the tide. Their
tender broke loose and fled off before the high wind, and the
poor wretches were unable to escape from the rush and haste of
the returning tide which rose and deepened about them. The
incident has a medieval quality. They kept firing off their guns,
but no one paid any attention to so familiar a sound. Well,
Heaven rest them all, poor souls.*

[To Dr. Neff]

We have bought a Hingham tree (said to have been cut in
Maine) and a box of Maine greens has been sent us. I have hung
one of the branches of fir balsam over an electric light fixture
and every time I see it, I utter low moans of recognition and
happiness—sounds like a moose nearing home. We came down
the day before Thanksgiving and ever since, I've led the existence
here of an exiled bear. More and more every year, this still
well-to-do, tidy (but beginning-to-be-vaguely-apprehensive)
suburb drives me nuts. There is no nature for a naturalist to see,
there are no birds save "the spotted Chevrolet and the Greater
and Lesser Buick"—that's one of my best and grimmest jokes!—
and the touch of Boston Harbor which lies in front of the house
and beyond the cars has absolutely no meaning to me in terms
of beauty and the spirit; it is nothing but a glacial spillover
surrounding a tub de mud.

NORTHERN FARM

[Groan of the Ice: Chapter Two]

Our house stands above a pond, a rolling slope of old fields leading down to the tumble and jumble of rocks which make the shore. We do not see the whole pond but only a kind of comfortable bay some two miles long and perhaps a mile or so across. To the south lies a country road, a wooded vale, and a great farm above on a hill; across and to the east are woods again and then a more rural scene of farms and open land. It is the north, and as I set down these words the whole country lies quiescent in the cup of winter's hand.

Last night, coming in from the barn, I stood awhile in the moonlight looking down toward the pond in winter solitude. Because this year winds have swept the surface clean of early snows, the light of the high and wintry moon glowed palely upwards again from a somber, even a black, fixity of ice. Nothing could have seemed more frozen to stone, more a part of universal silence.

All about me, too, seemed still, field and faraway stand of pine lying frozen in the motionless air to the same moonlit absence of all sound. Had I paused but a moment and then closed the door behind me, I probably would have spoken of the silence of the night. But I lingered a longish while, and lingering found that the seeming stillness was but the interval between the shuddering, the mysterious outcrying, of the frozen pond. For the pond was hollow with sound, as it is sometimes when the nights are bitter and the ice is free from snow.

It is the voice of solid ice one hears and not the wail and crash and goblin sighing of moving ice floes such as one hears on the wintry St. Lawrence below the Isle of Orleans. The sounds made by the pond are sounds of power moving in bondage, of force constrained within a force and going where it can. The ice is taking up, settling, expanding, and cracking across, though there is not a sign of all this either from the hill above or from the shore.

What I first heard was a kind of abrupt, disembodied groan. It came from the pond—and from nowhere. An interval of silence followed, perhaps a half note or a full note long. Then across, again from below, again disembodied, a long, booming, and hollow utterance, and then again a groan.

Again and again came the sounds; the night was still yet never still. Curiously enough, I had heard nothing while busy in the barn. Now, I heard. Neither faint nor heavy-loud, yet each one distinct and audible, the murmurs rose and ended and began again in the night. Sometimes there was a sort of hollow oboe sound, and sometimes a groan with a delicate undertone of thunder.

As I stood listening to the ice below, I became aware that I was really listening to the whole pond. There are miles of ice to the north and a shore of coves and bays, and all this ice was eloquent under the moon. Now east, now west, now from some far inlet, now from the cove hidden in the pines, the pond cried out in its strange and hollow tongue.

The nearer sounds were, of course, the louder, but even those in the distance were strangely clear. And save for this sound of ice, there seemed no other sound in all the world.

Just as I turned to go in, there came from below one curious and sinister crack which ran off into a sound like the whine of a giant whip of steel lashed through the moonlit air.

My old friends and neighbors, Howard and Agnes Rollins, used to tell me that the ice often spoke and groaned before a big storm. I must watch the glass and the wind and the northeast.

  The farm country is now a winter splendor of heavy woolens, a good, healthy spirited display of mackinaws in bright colors, cheerful plaid shirts, and heavy woolen caps of plaided red, green, or royal blue. The pageant is at its best when snow has fallen, and the bright colors move about against a universal white.

Some scholar has said, and very wisely, that the songs of a people are an excellent token of their character. The student of human nature would do well to add their clothes! Let him meditate on the fact that in peasant countries where the earth is the real wealth, and the farm lives by its own farm prides and farm traditions, the costumes worn are the most vital, beautiful, and gay that have ever been seen in western civilization.

Conversely, the clothes of an industrial world are the most dreary, ugly, muddy clothes that a way of living has ever put on human backs. Look at them as they are worn by any average urban crowd. There is no sense of hope in them, nothing of life in any mood of pride. Sartorially, this is a new thing in human history. From the noble savage onward, man has been something of a gay dog.

I am glad that the north country goes in for clothes with life and color. It is an excellent sign. Which reminds me that if the neighbors see me wearing a particularly gorgeous new pair of hand-knitted yellow socks, they can recognize a Christmas present arranged for by Elizabeth.

75

[*To David McCord*]

A moose recently walked down the main street of Damariscotta at an early hour of the morning.

And the odious hunters have shot a large, particularly genial bear—damn them!

*   *   *

We have had a first snow. It came at nightfall and was more sleet than snow, clicking at the panes like witches' fingernails, and volleying against the sides of the woodshed and the long, peaked roof in wild outbursts of wilder sound. Twice in the night, the inner house all still, the darkened world without all one vast fury, I got up to replenish the stoves—a figure in a red dressing gown going from one bed of coals to another, popping in generous billets to burn the rest of the night, and discretely tending to draughts and closing iron doors, fitting back lids. The next night, all stars and cold and lonely wildness, we had a fine show of Northern Lights over the new snow. By daylight, such a sifted whiteness brings out all the rusts and russets in a winter landscape. It was a day without birds.

[*To Ida R. Coatsworth, his mother-in-law*]

It was still, still and cold last night, and after I'd washed my dishes and given the room an evening fillip with the broom, I pulled the rocking chair over to the lamp and settled down to read a detective story I'd borrowed from the Days. It was just the kind of detective story I like, nothing about gunmen, American crooks, millionaires, and bootlegger kings, but about old London solicitors, an Elizabethan mansion, a trap door in the hearth, a mysterious somebody or something or other that killed people, and, far off in the fields, the family tombs.

It's winter here now, real winter, with the ground frozen, and every night the cold striking deeper down, with snow thin-strewn on the pale stubble, and the silence of the cold poised between land and sky. The clear days are beautiful; the nights magnificent with Northern Lights and burning stars.

[The Jays in Winter : Chapter Four]

It is the full midwinter, the season of snow, ear-tingling cold, and skies into whose blue the earth reflects back its own intensity of light. It is not heat but light which is returning to the world, and so glittering is the morning air and so cloudless the sky that the sun rolls up over the eastern woods like a sudden miracle of radiant gold, borrowing no red from the lower atmosphere.

No sound is more characteristic of this leafless time than the cries of blue jays from the nearer woods and the trees and buildings of the farm. Again and again, when I am busy out of doors, I hear that single screaming call across the wilderness of snow. I hear it just as the austere shadows of winter are coming to life with the sunrise, I hear it, and hear it answered, through the bright hollow of high noon. There is as yet no touch of spring in the note; it is the familiar harsh call and nothing more. Yet to us on the farms it is music, for it means that life in the air, daring, vigorous, and even jocular, is sharing the winter with us, and has not fled from us before the deep bitterness of cold.

I rarely see or hear them during January. But with February and the return of the light comes the flash of blue, and a first salute to the earth and the sun reborn.

77

Yesterday afternoon, while calling on a neighbor, I saw by his barn a sight I look for every year. He had been shaking hay down from his lofts, and had then taken his broom, and swept the chaff and hay-dust out upon the snow. The day was the very quintessence of the winter, a time of pure, universal blue and pure, universal white. In the full sunlight and the snow, my neighbor's neighbors had come to share the bounty of the barn. Five vigorous and gaudy jays were flying back and forth between a bit of fence rail adjoining the barn and the chaff-covered snow, a wonderful sight to see from scarcely ten feet away.

On the snow itself, prospecting and frisking in the chaff, their heads lowered, their bushy tails twitching, were two grey squirrels. Sometimes the jays and squirrels, grey fur and blue feathers all in company, were gathered together on the ground. Only once did I see the jays fly in a group to the fence top, and that was when the old farm cat passed them on her way into the barn. I could not see that she paid the slightest attention to the guests.

Ornithologists are given to scolding the jay, and accusing him of piratical behavior. We do not have the magpie in the east, but the jay is a close relative, and it is apt to be a rather mischievous family. But who could really be angry, and at such a time, with so handsome, "rugged," and American a bird? In a few weeks I should be hearing the spring note, that really musical and plaintive call which will mark the turning of the first corner of the year.

◢ᢶ The secret of snow is the beauty of the curve. In no other manifestation of Nature is the curve revealed in an almost abstract purity as a part of the visible mystery and splendor of the world. What I think of, as I set down these lines, is the intense and almost glowing line which a great dune of snow lifts against the blue radiance of the morning after a storm, that high, clear, and incomparable crest which is mathematics and magic, snow and the wind. How many times have I paused to stare at such a summit when I have found it barring my way at a turn of the unploughed country road! It is when winds are strong, temperatures low, and the snow almost powder-dry that you will see such monuments of winter at their best. Dunes of sand obey the same complex of laws, but the heavier sand does not have the aerial grace of the bodiless and radiant crystal which builds the snow against the sky.

[Winter Shadows : Chapter Six]

A strong and almost sandy crust has surfaced over the wintry countryside of snow. For three and even four steps, it bears one's weight like a white floor, and then, alas, it cracks, and one plunges through almost to the knee. As it is too glassy to be comfortable under snowshoes, and one cannot walk with much ease, we keep to our ploughed roads and shoveled paths and make the best of it. Held in its bright tension by the cold, and little troubled by the wind, the vast and shining floor is not without its own interest. For one thing, it is on such a surface that one can observe the shadows of winter, which are unlike all other shadows of the year.

Summer is the season of motion, winter is the season of form. In summer everything moves save the fixed and inert. Down the hill flows the west wind, making wavelets in the shorter grass and great billows in the standing hay; the tree in full leaf sways its heavy boughs below and tosses its leaves above; the weed by the gate bends and turns when the wind blows down the road. It is the shadow of moving things that we usually see, and the shadows are themselves in motion. The shadow of a branch,

speckled through with light, wavers across the lawn, the sprawling shadow of the weed moves and sways across the dust.

The shadows of winter are astronomical. What moves them is
the diurnal motion of the sun. The leafless tree may shudder
through its boughs, and its higher twigs and small branches sway
a little to and fro, but of that gaunt and rigid motion only a
ghost of movement trembles on the snow beneath. Tree-trunk
and tree shape, the birdhouse and its pole, the chimney with
its ceaseless smoke, the dead and nodding goldenrod—the life
of their shadows comes with sunrise and with sunset dies. All
day long beneath these winter suns, each austere and simplified
image slides glancingly from west to east with the slow and
ordained progress of the dial shadow on the wall.

Today having been spent outdoors from early morning to the
close of afternoon, it is these shadows I have been watching on
the hardened snow. They seem to me one of the most characteristic features of the winter, and I wonder that so little is said
about them by dwellers in the country.

Today's tree shadows began with the image long, aslant, and
blurred. The clearer and more definite shadow-image is always
near the trunk, close, that is, to the object by which the shadow
is cast. At noon, I thought, there came the maximum of defini-
tion. The sun is still rather low, and the shadow reached out
from the tree much more than it would in June. As the afternoon
lengthened, the shadows of the higher branches, always a little
blurred, grew more indistinct, leaning to the east. The whole
image died away on the snow in the winter twilight smoldering
in the cloud-haze to the west.

I have not the painter's eye, but I could see that the shadows
were blue even as the painters show them and that the blue
varied in intensity. That night, I went out awhile to watch the
moon shadows which again are astronomical, and thought certain

aspects of the tree images perhaps more definite than those I had seen by day.

The moon is now very high. Utterly silent, the huge landscape, glazed with the moon, rolled on under the heavens, the shadows foreshortened and falling due north. It might have been the phantom of a summer day.

৵§ The seed catalogues are arriving again, and as I take them down from their brown envelopes and study them at the kitchen table, I muse again on the dogmatic assertion which I often make that the countryman's relation to Nature must never be anything else but an alliance. Alas, I know well enough that Nature has her hostile moods, and I am equally aware that we must often face and fight as we can her waywardness, her divine profusion, and her divine irrationality. Even then, I will have it, the alliance holds. When we begin to consider Nature as something to be robbed greedily like an unguarded treasure, or used as an enemy, we put ourselves in thought outside of Nature, of which we are inescapably a part. Be it storm and flood, hail and fire, or the yielding furrow and the fruitful plain, an alliance it is, and that alliance is a cornerstone of our true humanity.

[To Dr. Neff]

Here we are at the old farm, with a whole deep world of purest white snow encompassing us about, the sun shining, Betsy B. and H.B. busy at the kitchen table, and a beef stew cooking on the stove in an old-fashioned stoneware beanpot. The coal stove is busily at its job, the kitchen range talks to itself with the soft flutter of fire and the boiling sound of the cooking stew. There is a good deal of discomfort in the village itself (Damariscotta) among those who are heating their homes with coal, and they are freezing themselves by day in order to save their water pipes at night. We found one family running all their fireplaces, and assembling as one around a Franklin which was behaving like a hero. But if John L. Lewis appeared, he would be smothered and covered over with old and frozen lobster bait or tossed into these icy seas! Temperature today—minus 4°. Cold, yes, but how quiet, peaceful and beautiful it is. We have been on long snowshoe hikes into the woods, and various groups of friends have called, bringing their snowshoes with them, and pots and pots of coffee on the stove!

It is always like having a second Christmas when one returns here, after having been absent for some weeks. The post office is up to its neck in package mail, books mostly, though it is agreeably miscellaneous, and the stack of British and American magazines, reviews, gift-copies and whatnot would fill a barn. The torn-off paper just fills the whole dining room. So we luxuriate in literatoor! I get up at 6 to restoke and rebuild the fires, make coffee, and start breakfast, and so far we have fared well. I am reading up on astronomy at the moment.

[To his wife]

Another blizzard, less rainy than the last one, but every bit as wild. Just the kind of storm, I should say, that Lucy Gray was lost in. It is so thick at the far edges that you can see scarce a quarter of a mile anywhere: beyond that distance lies a furious, North Dakota whiteness. Very little sound.

Supper: pancakes and maple syrup, henceforth classical fare for any blizzard night. Still snowing, the small flakes being felt as a cold wetness driving against the cheeks.

Nine: I have just been out for a walk with Lawrence, snowshoeing in the beautiful moonlit night. The moon itself

*is concealed and it is snowing hard, but the disk is only one day
from the full and all this world is drenched in storm and lunar
beauty.*

[From Chapter Five]

ⲉ§ One aspect of the machine world which has not had suf-
ficient attention is the relation of the machine age to the mystery
of human joy. If there is one thing clear about the centuries
dominated by the factory and the wheel, it is that although the
machine can make everything from a spoon to a landing-craft,
a natural joy in earthly living is something it never has and
never will be able to manufacture. It has given us conveniences
(often most uncomfortable) and comforts (often most incon-
venient) but human happiness was never on its tray of wares.
The historical result of the era has been an economic world so
glutted with machine power that it is being shaken apart like a
jerry-built factory, and a frustrate human world full of neurotic
and ugly substitutes for joy.

Part of the confused violence of our time represents, I think,
the unconscious search of man for his own natural happiness. He
cannot live by bread alone and particularly not by sawdust bread.
To speak in paradox, a sense of some joy in living is one of the
most serious things in all the world.

[*To Mrs. F. Morton Smith, his sister-in-law*]

*Yes, there at the station, wearing his red plaid winter jacket and
the huge boots of this countryside, stood Carroll winking his
paw, and then the farm, genially red, a vast slope of white, with a
little smoke curling from the chimneys. The house comfortable*

83

as ever, the new kitchen pump a treasure worthy of an Emperor, and the dark coming clear and not too cold and the evening star appearing golden somewhere above the barn.

Last night we had an ice storm to coat the trees, our prize exhibit being Johnny the weathervane man, who was seen this morning riding the sky on a crystal steed, with four aerial icicles hanging one from each hoof, and one midway from the tail, and the rider himself, a little man of bright diamond, facing the comfortable glare of the Sunday morning sun. The youngish pines look just like court ladies of the eighteenth century in big, billowy, green and crystal gowns, with the plume atop for their fantastic headdresses. One lonely glade here, all aglitter in the blue sky and the sun, looked like a ballet.

[From Chapter Seven]

⋙ The chromium millennium ahead of us, I gather, is going to be an age whose ideal is a fantastically unnatural human passivity. We are to spend our lives in cushioned easy chairs, growing indolent and heavy while intricate slave mechanisms do practically everything for us as we loll.

What a really appalling future! What normal human being would choose it, and what twist of the spirit has created this sluggish paradise? No, I do not mean that we should take the hardest way. Compromises are natural and right. But a human being protected from all normal and natural hardship simply is not alive.

[Winter Stars : Chapter Eight]

Supper has been cleared away, the dishes done, and the peaceful, lamplit kitchen restored to its evening simplicity. Because the night was cold, we lingered by the cozier fire, Elizabeth deep in a book, and I going through those agricultural papers and magazines which had arrived for me since the beginning of the month. I am rather given to letting such mail accumulate, and saving the reading for a quiet night. Just as I was in the middle of an article, I remembered something I had forgotten in the barn. As there was nothing to do but go out and see to it, I shouldered into my blue reefer, picked up my lantern and turned to the door. And closing it behind me, I walked out into another world.

It was a night such as one sees perhaps half a dozen times a winter. The sky was less a sky of earth than interstellar space itself revealed in its pure and overarching height, an abyss timeless and remote and sown with an immense glittering of stars in their luminous rivers and pale mists, in their solitary and unneighbored splendors, in their ordered figures, and dark, half-empty fields. It was the middle of the evening and in the north over a lonely farm, a great darkness of the forest, and one distant light, the Dipper, stood on its handle, each star radiant in the blue and empty space about the pole.

These are the seven stars which come and go through the ages and the religions. Collectively known to the medieval past by the fine name of "The Plough," the configuration is today the Great Dipper to beholders, and gathered thus into a household and utilitarian shape, places something of our small humanity in the shoreless oceans of the sky.

The greater splendor burned white and blue above the south. There exalted and assembled in one immense principality of the skies, the shining press of the greater winter constellations glittered above the little cold and dark of earth. Orion, most beautiful of all the stellar figures, shone beyond the meridian, the timeless hunter of the timeless sky, Betelgeuse and Bellatrix burning on his shoulders and the triad of the belt about his waist. Sirius, lord of the ancient Nile and brightest of the stars, hung in his glorious and solitary place, the Bull with the reddened eye of Aldebaran charged some invader of his field of suns, and the matched stars of Gemini together with the planets Mars and Saturn formed themselves into a figure which astrologers might have watched and questioned through the night.

One stares awhile and then looks to earth for the reassurance which comes with the earthly and the near. What was left of a light snow lay starlit and pale, the vague and ragged regions of uncovered earth starlit too, yet half lost in the dark. Fixed in such a starlit gloom, the barn raised its shadowy bulk to the light and the mystery overhead. In the more empty sky below Sirius, scattered stars shone through the branches of trees beside the road.

It was as I came from the barn that I saw agriculture standing like a good omen above the fields. The starry plough had vanished from the imagination and the common language of man, but the remembered sickle stood high in the south and east and moved towards the meridian. Rolling on with all celestial space, the Lion of the zodiac followed great Orion, the fine if albeit left-handled sickle which the stars form glittering in the abyss, and at the base of the handle the great star Regulus, white, splendid, and serene.

Lower still, a new light trembled on the wooded ridge. It was Arcturus bringing with him that assurance of the spring and dedication of time for which the ancients used to wait in their warmer lands, Arcturus the great, the yellow star, loved of so many generations of men who live by bread.

◆§ How wise were the ancients who never lost sight of the religious significance of the earth! They used the land to the full, draining, ploughing, and manuring every inch, but their use was not an attack on its nature, nor was the ancient motherhood of earth ever forgotten in the breaking and preparing of the soil.

They knew, as all honest people know in their bones, that in any true sense there is no such thing as ownership of the earth and that the shadow of any man is but for a time cast upon the grass of any field. What remains is the earth, the mother of life as the ancients personified the mystery, the ancient mother in her robes of green or harvest gold and the sickle in her hand.

When farming becomes purely utilitarian, something perishes. Sometimes it is the earth life which dies under this "stand and deliver" policy; sometimes it is the human beings who practice this economy, and oftenest of all it is a destruction of both land and man. If we are to live and have something to live for, let us remember, all of us, that we are the servants as well as the masters of our fields.

[From Chapter Ten]

ও§ No age in history can afford to lay too much emphasis upon "security." The truth is that from our first breath to our last we inhabit insecurely a world which must of its transitory nature be insecure, and that moreover any security we do achieve is but a kind of an illusion. While admitting that a profound instinct towards such safety as we can achieve is part of our animal being, let us also confess that the challenge involved in mere existence is the source of many of the greater virtues of human character.

[From Chapter Eleven]

ও§ A few days before the Vernal Equinox we have a kind of special celebration in the farm kitchen and at breakfast time. The kitchen, as I have said, is in the ell of the house, and because on one side the windows face due east, we have for the greater part of the year the awakening and refreshing presence of the morning sun. As October draws near, the great disk, moving south, with every sunrise draws nearer a corner of the main house extended beyond the ell and cutting off our view to the southeast.

Nearer and nearer to the fated corner moves the great lamp, nearer and nearer, turns it, and the kitchen does not have morning sunlight till long months have worn away.

If we were people of the Golden Age and the Golden Bough, we would get our pipes and timbrels, our long trumpets of bronze, and our other musical what-have-you's ready for March fifteenth. On that morning the sun, which has been steadily approaching the corner, turns it, the golden round rising clear of all obstruction and flooding the kitchen with the first spring light. It is for us an occasion of real joy. We may not belong to the Golden Age or the years of the Golden Bough, but we can observe and rejoice, and in such natural joy and natural response lies one of the profoundest secrets of human happiness.

[To his wife]

Walking with a lantern in the nine o'clock darkness, the night sky was a dark ghostliness of broken romantic cloud with light along the edges of breaking, a light that might have been a ghostly moonlight, yet there was no moon. On the earth, darkness of field and tree, darkness of lake water, and a silence so indwelling that I could hear the thin whisper of the blood in my ears. Suddenly, a loon began to call, a distant ululation, and calling again and again with long pauses of silence between was answered by a loon in Deep Cove, the fine wild sound coming to us distantly under the motionless, islanded sky and across the somber heights of the trees.

[The Spring Waters : Chapter Thirteen]

It has always been our custom to take a little stroll before we put the house to bed, merely going to the gate and back when the nights are hostile with a bitterness of cold. Now that nights more mercifully human have come with the slow and dilatory spring, we go beyond the gate for perhaps a quarter or even half a mile, walking with miry feet down the farm road and through a sound of many waters.

Tonight under a faintly hazy sky and through a light wind one can feel but not hear, the winter is flowing downhill towards the still frozen and imprisoned pond. Out of the forests and the uplands a skein of rills is pouring, the small streams now seeking their ancient courses, now following an hour's new runnel along the darkness of a wall.

If the opening music of the northern year begins with a first trumpet call of the return of light, and the return of warmth is the second great flourish from the air, the unsealing of the waters of earth is certainly the third. As we walked tonight in a darkness from which a young moon had only just withdrawn, the earth everywhere, like something talking to itself, murmured and even sang with its living waters and its living streams.

Between us and the gate, a torrent as from an overflowing spring, half blocked by a culvert heaved by frost, chided about our feet, and making another and smaller sound found its way downhill again in the night. Farther on, where woods close in to one side and the ground is stony and uneven, there tinkled out of the tree shapes and the gloom a sound of tiny cascades falling with incessant flow into a pool together with the loud and musical plashing of some newborn and unfamiliar brook.

Cold and wet, the smell in the spring air was not yet the smell of earth and spring. No fragrance of the soil, no mystery of vernal warmth hung above the farmland, but only a chill of sodden earth, water, and old snow. I knew that if I cared to look, I could find to the north of weathered ledges in the woods such sunken, grey-dirty, and gritty banks of ice as only the spring rains find and harry from the earth.

Yet spring somehow was a part of the night, the miry coldness, and the sound of water, a part of this reluctance of winter to break camp, a part of these skies with Sirius and Orion ready to vanish in the west. The long siege was broken, the great snows were over and gone, the ice was coming down from above tidewater in the current of the great rivers, and the colored twigs of the trees were at last awake.

Walking homewards toward the farm, now listening to the sound of water, now forgetting it as we talked, we both could see that much of the pond was surfaced with open water above its floor of ice. At the foot of our own hayfields a cove facing south and east showed in liquid and motionless dark, whilst beyond, and again above the ice, lay puddles and seas whose reflected quiet of starshine was a promise of the open water soon to come.

Across the pools, at the great farm on the hill, a light suddenly went out. Our own windows shone near by, but we did not enter, so haunted were we both by the sense of the change in the year and the continuous sound of waters moving in the earth.

When we at length entered the house, using the side door and its tramped-over and muddy step, we found ourselves welcomed by something we are very seldom aware of summer or winter—the country smell of the old house.

All old farms, I imagine, have some such rustic flavor in their walls; country dwellers will recognize what I mean. A hundred and fifty years of barreled apples, of vegetables stored in a fieldstone cellar, of potatoes in the last of the spring, of earth somewhere and never very far, of old and enduring wood and woodsmoke, too, and perhaps the faintest touch of mold from things stored long, long ago in a bin—all these and heaven knows what other farmhouse ghosts were unmistakably present in the neat room with its lamp and books. The cold and humid night had stirred the house as well as ourselves: it had its own rustic memories.

Elizabeth presently brought in two slices of apple pie and two glasses of cold milk, and for a first time I did not bother to build up the fire.

⊷§ The city has its heat and cold, its hunger and its thirst, but it has lost a great measure of the human birthright of physical sensation. Life there is so protected from nature, so insulated, so to speak, that it ends up by being only a ghost of the human adventure. I say this because it has always seemed to me that a normal range of physical sensation, a sense, for instance, of the fabric of earth underfoot and the sudden cold of a change of the wind, is not only a part of the discipline of life but also of its reward.

[To his brother-in-law]

Under this warm air, under this pleasant sky, the obstinate earth remains as wan and pale as if it had emerged but yesterday from under February's snow. Who shall convince these grey ledges, these rusty junipers, these sodden pastures lifted and hubble-bubbled by the frost, that their six months of winter are over and done and that "the voice of the turtle is heard in the land"?

*Only the lake seems to have heard. A week ago, the ice sheet
had receded from the shore, leaving a winding path of open
water between its edges and the land. Within this girdle of
darker water lay the continent of ice itself, treacherous-looking,
and rain-colored, a world of grey. Then open water began to
appear to the leeward of islands and capes; soon the open places
were larger than the ice, and at the end of a lovely warm day
the surface was clear. There was no wind this time to break up
the ice. It melted away like ice from a window pane; one looked
in the morning, it was there; one looked in the evening, and
there was the lake twinkling away as if nothing had happened
all the winter long. And that night the geese came back, a great
flock of them flying down the north and south channel of the
lake, crossing the sky at sundown with multitudinous cries and
a great rushing sound of wings. Far away dogs began to bark,
and then all sounds died away, and I heard the sound of our own
spring running its delicate treble in the advancing night.*

[The Geese Return : Chapter Fifteen]

Three days of warmish spring weather and three days of bottom-
less mud, and now comes a morning of cold and glaring light
with the northwest wind blowing the chimney smoke of the
wood fires. The pine branches on the pasture hill roll and sway,
the tops of the trees restlessly nodding, and over the dead grass
fly last year's oak leaves in their familiar panic before the invisible streaming of the air.

The wind is neither high nor keen, it is only blustery and
comfortably cold. Out of the region of the sky called "the eye
of the wind" it comes, and looking thither, I see there a blue
clarity and even a cold luminousness as of a window into outer
space.

Over the grass, over the roofs and the house, the eddies gather and sweep on, each great sigh trailing behind it a silence which is never a full hush. Only the pond remains in grim quiescence. Still frozen, it lies at the foot of our slopes like an obstinate nugget of winter, the ever-thinning surface changing color with the depth of ice, the vagaries of temperature, and the differing hues of the sky.

The winter's two-foot floor was no such mirror, and under any sky had an austere look which was all its own. But this ice! Yesterday morning, after a sharp night, the pond emerged from the darkness a new and glassy white, a milk-onyx white, and this it kept till early afternoon when it took on a greyness of mush snow. By evening it had gone steely, darkening to another strange color without any quality or vibration of life.

Obstinate relic of winter, when will it be gone? Not "till the pond is open" will this cold and muddy earth waken to its own life under the already awakened sky. There is a country saying here, and a sound one, that the frost is never fully out of the ground till the ice is out of the pond. When will it go this year? When will it turn that strange blue which is the signal of its disappearance? I have seen the pond open on the twenty-sixth of March—the earliest date anyone can remember—I have seen it stay frozen till April was almost at its end.

Had I not stopped yesterday to study the pond, to "stand and stare" as Davies says, I would have missed something I hope to have a sight of every spring.

Friends had told me that the geese were going north. My neighbor Elwell Oliver saw a flock go over March fifteenth, a little after midday. Another neighbor whose farm is on a hill heard them last week "hollering" overhead as he went to his barn in the early dark. Because our lakes are frozen, the geese here follow the coast, and settle down for a spell in the open, salt water estuaries and tidal reaches of our great freshwater streams. I have seen them by the hundreds in the coves and sheltered by-waters of the Kennebec and the Penobscot, making themselves at home there well on towards the end of spring.

There is a kind of sixth sense which gives one a nudge now and then, and it was probably that sense which prompted me to look at the sky while I was studying the pond. The geese had come from behind, from the west-southwest, and there they were, just overhead, in a sky without a single cloud, in a sky all light and springtime blue. It was a large flock, and the birds were flying rather high in a marked but irregular "V." I heard no "hollering," not a note of that lovely, bell-like chorusing which so stirs the heart when a great flock of Canada geese go over in the early night.

Over the pond they went and on towards a ridge lying almost due northeast. I could see them as they cleared it, melting away in the sky above the farms and trees as a faint and wavering line. I looked at my watch; it was a few minutes after four o'clock, and the shadows on the steely lake were themselves turning steely on the ice.

⊷§ There is one principle which our world would do well to remember, for it is of first importance whether one sharpens a pencil, builds a house, bakes bread, or lays the intended foundations for Utopia. It is this—that what we make is conditioned by the means we use making it. We may have the best intentions in the world, but if we sharpen our pencils with a dull knife or build a house with a faulty rule, the pencil will be badly sharpened and the house will have an odd little way of opening doors by itself and leaning to one side.

In our barn the larger beams were worked over and squared by someone using what was probably an old-fashioned shipbuilder's axe. They are honestly and carefully made, and something of the humanity of the past is in them to this day. Certain other beams have been sawed out, and they are good beams, too, although quite different in look and feeling. The means used in making have marked each kind of beam for all time.

But I do not wish to labor the point. It is enough to say that prophets of expedience who are careless of the means they use and who work outside the human and moral values, have never been able to build anything humanly worth while.

[To his wife]

Cold again, and praise God for that, for the road was, as the fat boy who bought the hay said, "a caution." It was April all over, but a sudden and not-quite-ready-for-it April; and the road, or rather the geographical delimitations of a road, was a long course of appalling muck in whose deeper gulfs I distinctly saw the roofs of China. You must imagine a slough no less, of mud just soft and plasticine-ish enough to keep its shape, all ridged, rutted, gullied, and masticated by such desperate motorists as ventured its despond. I just about got home, having gone to Damariscotta to get some quite necessary oil. Yes, said the fat boy—"She's a caution!"

The other day was again a day of that terrifying silence I wrote of, of that vast stillness which the interpreter can only render in negatives, "no stir of leaf or sound of any bird"—"and no birds sing." I am beginning to see something here which I was familiar with upon the Cape, the sight of rafts of wildfowl. Yesterday there was a fine flock of "red-heads," today (comfortably out in the bay) there is a gathering of several hundred duck of some kind, and so thick massed are they

95

*that, to the leeward of them, the water lies in a quiet slick.
There is ice on the lake again, floating like broken scum of
milk on a pot.*

[From Chapter Sixteen]

⮜§ On a dark and none too warm evening, the alder swamp
rings with the triumphant chorus of a whole nation of spring
peepers. The living, exultant noise sounds like a frenzy of tiny
sleighbells, and through it one hears the musical trilling of the
common toad, and the occasional jug-o'-rum of a bull frog.
Heard near by, the din from the swamp is almost deafening. It
is a Dionysian ecstasy of night and spring, a shouting and a re-
joicing out of puddles and streams, a festival of belief in sheer
animal existence.

What has come over man that he has so lost this animal faith?
If he wishes to stay alive as a creature of earth, it is to this faith
that he must cling at all possible cost, for let him once relax his
hold, out of his own being will emerge that brood of pessimisms
and despairs which will bend back his fingers till they have
broken his hold on life, and with it his vital and primitive
strength. The body is not all of us, though a metaphorical
animal carries us all upon its back, and even as the body keeps
its own mysterious wills—even such as that of the heart to beat—
so must it have its own appropriate and earthly faith. It was a
fine music from the marsh, and in these our times I wish that
all the world had been there to hear.

[*To David McCord*]

*Saw two eagles yesterday, building a nest. Back and forth across
the sea woods they flew, each huge bird carrying an actual bundle*

96

of sticks. They might have been scouts gathering wood for an outdoor fire. What's more, the bundles were fairly sizeable.

*   *   *

All morning long, an enormous porcupine has been grubbing about in the level hayfield to the west of the house, and scarce a long stone's throw from this window pane. As he moves about in the dead grass, he seems to move exactly as does a toy mouse; you remember them?—they moved on a spool and a spring, and their life-line was a long thread of rubber. People used to sell them on the sidewalks.

Late spring is full of melancholy here. There is no lift of the heart; it is no time for timbrels and dances, for boys and girls with flutes, and for the goddess Flora—"the lovely Roman"— drawn by oxen in a painted car. Winter has withdrawn as a tide withdraws, leaving the winter-tidal forlornness and wreckage behind on the figurative beach of the landscape. It might be November, save that the wind is warm. If lyric poetry streams from a lyric mood, how little there is of truly lyric in this Red Indian north! The lyric mood is hard to find in America. The seasonal procession isn't dramatized for it, and the air is too tense.

[Rainy Day in the Kitchen : Chapter Eighteen]

A spell of cold and rainy weather from the North Atlantic drifts inland across the drenched and cheerless coast; thin fog blurs the distant reaches of the pond, and a light wind which never dies down blows sudden drizzles of rain against the windows to the east. It is a day for a huge, reassuring open fire, but our kitchen fireplace being still blocked with its fire-front and the winter stove, we have to content ourselves with keeping a good

97

fire burning in the range. The successive showers are almost soundless, but I am aware of them as they come because with each arrival the tinkle of the cistern inflow grows louder under the boards of the kitchen floor. The only other real sound is that of the kettle beginning a humming sigh from the back of the range, a mild, contented, and indoor music very appropriate to the day.

As I write, the kitchen clock tells me that it is the middle of the afternoon, and presently comes rain in a real shower. Although I have been held back all day from various tasks outside, I find my mind content to stay under a roof on so cheerless an afternoon. It is on such a day that one comes to feel and appreciate the personality of one's house, and that "the house spirit," as the Chinese say, seems in a mood to tell what it has to tell. If the house is an old one, and has been cherished, a real sense of the past comes to life within the walls and the window panes. A hundred and twenty-five years have passed like cloud shadows over this roof since young men raised the timber above the field-stone cellars and the boulders at the corners, for well over a hundred years the touch of human life has smoothed the house as the flowing of a brook wears smooth a pebble in the current of the stream. Every outer threshold, for instance, shows the scooped hollow of the footsteps of those who have come and gone down the archways of the years.

Elizabeth says, "Say of it first that it is a kind house." There are no patches which catch and trip the passer-by, no beams or corners which bump unwary heads, no latches or gadgets which pinch the fingers. It has no architectural malices which lie in wait.

It is perhaps in the kitchen that one is most aware of the human past, for the kitchen, even as it is now, was the center of existence of the farm. In this room and before the great fireplace assembled the young married men who cleared the land and the first fields, the men and their sons who cleared the larger fields and the pasture hill, the countrymen who shaped the fine timbers of the barn with the shipbuilders' axe, and the women of the farm who did the cooking, the weaving, the knitting, and kept the household together. They must have been a hardy lot to have stood these winters without stoves. Wheat flour was scarce in the frontier north in those ancient days, and neighbors tell me that it was barley bread and rye bread and corn-cake which were baked in the brick ovens and in the iron skillets to one side of the living fire.

I once had a glimpse of the room as it might have been in the early nineteenth century. There had come to work with us a young Passamaquoddy Indian, and it came about that one October night we left the farm in his care and went forth to have supper with friends. The boy could neither read nor write, and when his work was done, he simply relaxed in a rocking chair and took things in a kind of restful blank.

When we returned a little before eleven, I noticed as we drove in that the lamps in the kitchen had all been turned very low. Where was Roland, for that was our Indian's very un-Indian name? Entering the kitchen quietly, we came upon a scene the farm will long remember. The boy had taken an old blanket from his bed, rolled up in it, stretched himself longwise on the floor before the dying fire, and gone to sleep. Even thus his Indian ancestors had made themselves at home at some colonial neighbor's. The old Yankee kitchen, the darkness, and the drowsy fire, the tanned out-of-door young face—it was the past and pure romance. I hated to wake him, but I did so, and with the ceremonious politeness which was a part of his spirit, he took his candle, said a proper good night, and went to bed. I wish I knew what has become of him. Wherever he is, the farm wishes him well.

99

۵§ In spite of rain and cloud, the spring draws near. In the wet and dripping trees, even on these forlorn afternoons, the robins have managed the beginnings of a song. With the change, there comes something particularly needed by the human spirit—an affirmation of that eternal change in nature which rules out stagnancy, and the appearance of the entirely new within the pattern of the old. We are not treated to fantasies and monsters; the world remains the world we have known. I suspect that in human existence our problem is the finding of some like harmony between what is fixed and of the pattern and what is untried and eager to be born.

[*To his wife*]

The mason is a cheerful, apple-faced man with quiet ways and a hand for stone; rocks and boulders obey him as he were Prospero, and you have a cromlech wall under your house while you are writing a letter. He works with his son, a youngster of about medium height with monstrously strong shoulders and great muscular arms—a kind of a blend of a Maine Indian and the Farnese Hercules when nineteen years old, and it was a Doric sight to see them working quietly and contentedly in the valley of the boulders: the rhythm of human strength and the rhythm of stone.

What we have wanted for children is here, and is here in beauty and plenty, earth, air, fire, and water. I do so want our household to know the realities of earthly living—the earth under the plough, the stir and rustle of corn in the wind, the sound and the taste of purely running water, and the hunger of fire for the stored-away branch. All these are here. The farm is really two places. There's a family farm with running water and sinks and an oil stove and an oil heater for baths and the hot water tank. And then there is the old farm with its cistern

100

*economy and its sink and its big wood stove and its lamps and
candles and fireside baskets of lichened winter hardwood. They
exist, not exactly side by side, but complementarily.*

[From Chapter Twenty]

ᴥᔓ It often strikes me that in our modern Babylons you never
see anything begin. Everything comes to you, even thought, at
a certain stage of its development, like an iceberg lettuce. Now
life is more a matter of beginnings than of endings, and without
some sense of the beginning of things, there is no proper perspective on the whole mystery of living. This is only one detail,
but it will serve as one of the marks of the whole incomplete
urban perspective in which we live. For the city governs us now
as never before; it tells us what to love and what to hate, what
to believe and what not to believe, and even what to make of
human nature.

I begin to suspect that we should be more on our guard
against Babylon when its urbanism has gone bloodless and sterile,
and it insists on our taking its false maps of the human adventure. We must regain the truer and fuller perspective, one
leading back to origins and to beginnings human, earthy, concealed, and slow. No map is worth a penny which does not
include both the city and the fields.

[*To his wife*]

*I hasten to chronicle a minor but quite interesting adventure.
Last night, about 8:30, as we were all of us returning from a
visit to a friend of Jake's in Jake's car, a car coming towards us,
on its own side, slowed down and stopped abruptly, and Jake,*

who was driving, stopped as well. There then rose from the obscurity on the ground between us an ungainly struggling something which, getting to its feet in the cross-glare, stood revealed as a cow moose! She was scarce the length of our living room away from us, and she had not been struck, thank heaven, but only confused. They are curious, hobbledehoy creatures anyhow, and it was really quite moving to see this huge wild thing thus revealed. Across our lights she passed, and over the road brim to a lawn, and across a big farmyard to a back lot and the woods, there to be lost in the night. I think she was carrying a calf, and was grateful that there were no dogs to plague her.

And good news. The huge pileated woodpeckers—magnificent birds!—are building in our woods, in a dead tree standing solitary in the slash.

Our spring is superb now that it is cleaned out. The water man says that he has never seen a more pure and beautiful flow of water, and that the spring-well he is building will be the only one he knows of where the four sides go down to a bed of natural stone with the water pouring from the actual stone! A regular brooklet now flows downhill towards the lake. The country folk have all heard of it and came wandering by all day yesterday to look at it and exclaim. Mr. Childs came in, a charming little old Mainer eighty years old, of the shipbuilding line. He told me of his father's and his aunt's rescue from a sinking ship in the Mediterranean, effected by an English brig, and of how they manoeuvred their topsails in some tricky sailor fashion to keep the ships abreast, and of how the foundering State-of-Mainer went down with her topsail set.

*   *   *

Yesterday to the alewife stream on a coldish day following a warm one, to find a few sluggish, explorative fish, most of them gathered in congeries of fifty or so in the quiet water of the lower levels, and seemingly making no effort to climb.

102

[The Alewives : Chapter Twenty-three]

I have just returned from a visit to Damariscotta Mills and the alewife run. Every year we all go over to see this great run of fish which is one of the marvels of our coast.

Some three miles away as the crow flies, the long, narrow arm of our pond flows south to a natural dam some fifty feet high, and there winds and tumbles down a stairway of cascades into the salt water of a tidal bay. The glen of the cascades is such a scene as one might find in an old Currier and Ives print or imagine for oneself out of Thoreau's America—a glen, a vale, of old rocks and tall, peaceful elms, of the incessant sound of waterfalls, and the white wings of seagulls coming and going, going and coming, far above and in the blue. Old houses have closed in to one side, their shingles forever wet with spray where they stand above the water, and the open windows of their kitchens and sheds forever full of the beautiful, incessant sound of the pouring streams.

It is to these waters that the alewives come every spring, going up to the pond to spawn from their unknown winter refuge in the outer sea. Although we call such runs here "herring runs," the fish is not a true herring though it resembles one in size and shape. Our word "alewife" is a sort of early colonial transformation into English sound of an Indian word used by the red men of seventeenth-century Massachusetts, and carried Downeast by early settlers of our towns.

Perhaps a million or so fish crowd and swarm into the bay. They arrive in April, and their presence in the salt river is signaled to us by a simultaneous arrival of fishing birds from all our region of the coast. The gulls come, a cloud of wings and hungry cries, the fierce osprey finds himself a shelter and a watchtower, and the fiercer and piratic eagle comes to take the osprey's catch. The fish show no haste in going up into the pond.

103

The living mass waits for good weather, and for a new warmth in the outlet stream. On some fine morning in May, with the sun shining overhead, the run begins.

Entering from the bay, the thickly crowding, blue-backed, golden-bellied masses are confronted by a channel which branches at the dam into two wild, out-rushing brooks. One stream leads to the cascades and to wooden basins from which the alewives are dipped in nets and sent to the smokehouse, for there is an ancient commerce in these fish between our villages and the West Indian isles. It is probably the last relic of the eighteenth-century economy of colonial America. The other stream leads to a winding stair of old fieldstone basins built well over a hundred years ago to help the run move up into the pond.

Built as ruggedly as our boulder walls and mellowed now by water and the years, these basins on the slope interpose their twistings and turnings to the furious descent of one branch of the outlet stream and at the top lead out of crying foam and currents into the mild and quiet haven of the pond.

The day being warm and summerish and the tide high in the morning, there was a fine run moving upstream when I arrived. One could see the unnumbered mass moving in from the bay, and holding its own in the strong current of fresh water, a stream of life battling an opposing stream. There was a touch of lavender in the blue-black color of the massed fish as they swam under the skin of the brown and rippled water, the swarm pressing close together, each fish having just room to move its fins and no more.

Above and in the channel of the basins the stream was all a miracle of water and life, of life pressing onward, struggling fiercely to turn, climbing, climbing through the wild watery roar and the torrent whose foam was swift with the shadow and sunlight of the elms overhead, life pressing on, believing in itself, keeping the first faith, and remembering the immemorial decree.

◆§ Among the many things for which I remain profoundly grateful is the fact that so much of life defies human explanation. The unimaginative and the dull may insist that they have an explanation for everything, and level at every wonder and mystery of life their pop-gun theories, but, God be praised, their wooden guns have not yet dislodged the smallest star. It is well that this be so, for the human spirit can die of explanations, even if, like many modern formulae, they are but explanations which do not explain.

A world without wonder, and a way of mind without wonder, becomes a world without imagination, and without imagination man is a poor and stunted creature. Religion, poetry, and all the arts have their sources in this upwelling of wonder and surprise. Let us thank God that so much will forever remain out of reach, safe from our inquiry, inviolate forever from our touch.

[The Birds : Chapter Twenty-four]

Perhaps in all our country scene, nothing seems more eager and living than the birds. Because this is old forest country only here and there opened into farms, we have a rather large variety of species. Among them are birds of the northern woods, birds of the farm country, birds who like pond shores, water birds, and even strays from the neighboring Atlantic. You never can tell what you may see. Two years ago, for instance, that fantastic creature, the northern pileated woodpecker, flew out of the woods and rested for a while on the ridgepole of our disused icehouse, and only last fall, going down to the fields after a wild Northeaster, I startled up a red-legged guillemot from between the blown, disheveled rows of corn. It was a strange sight to see that ocean creature flying through inland Maine.

105

Certain birds we can count on as familiars. Robins are our songsters, cheerfully loquacious and musically talkative from the nearer trees, sociable heralds of the early light, and builders of nests in absurd places. Last year a robin who would have had difficulties with an intelligence test, built a nest under the big tank on a beam exposed to the deluges of the frequent overflows. The farm wondered if she planned to raise ducks! Chimney swifts have built in the chimney of my bedroom, and sometimes wake me in the early morning with the muffled and hollow roaring of their wings as they flutter up from their cavern of night and soot into the air of dawn.

The usual yellow warblers are at home in a sheltered apple tree whose branches shade the house, the usual catbirds are in their chokecherry thicket, and the tree swallows have again taken over the birdhouse which needs a coat of paint. The barn swallows, too, have come, and for the time being are hunting in the air above and about the house, on tireless wings darting and glancing high above the old apple tree in flower, the red water tank, and the two tall, austere chimneys of the ell. In the quiet evenings after sundown we hear the thrushes calling from the woods.

If these are the familiars of the house, the hilltop, and the barn, the bobolink is the very spirit of the fields. These slopes rolling down to the pond are a bobolink paradise, and all summer long we live in sight and sound of them, the fields housing perhaps a dozen or even twenty pairs. The male birds arrive in the middle of May, and the females follow soon after. As my old friend Edward Forbush once wrote, "The bobolink is the harlequin of the fields, and he wears his suit wrong-side up." Again and again here, I have watched him pursue his mate, singing as he goes, the bubbling song and the purposeful, determined flight joined together in one exultant surge of living. Nests are built on the ground and are hidden with particular skill in tangles at the foot of bushy weeds and near clumps of taller grass.

The eggs once laid, the female takes charge of housekeeping, leaving the male free to celebrate his song while keeping a weather eye on the nest in case of trouble. June is our bobolink month, and it is the feast of song we are now hearing. From branches of nearby trees, from fence posts, from some swaying weed top, from the living air, the bobolink song pours downward through space like the sound of some musical waterfall. Sometimes when I am working in the kitchen garden, I lay down my trowel just to listen awhile.

⁓§ Under today's disorders there is something at work among the nations whose great importance has not yet been adequately realized—the need of men for a community to live in and live with. The hope is vague, unsaid, and unformulated, but the need is great, and there is something in our hearts which troubles us that we have lost what was once so beautifully called "the commonweal."

I suspect that if this open wound is to heal, it will have to heal like all wounds from the bottom, and that we shall have to begin at the beginning with the family and its obligations, with the village and its responsibilities, and with our universal and neglected duty to the earth.

[To his wife]

Saw a rather lovely and unusual thing last night. I went into a little local greenhouse to get a geranium, and found it empty of everything save flowers, the last of the afternoon light, and the busiest of hummingbirds. There was an aisle of raspberry and white petunias to one side, and from flower to flower he hummed, darting his bill into calyx after calyx, thrusting his sharp self into the flowers with electrical rapidity (I hate the metaphor, but it gives something of the instantaneousness and

*the jeweled violence) and making long zooms scarce a foot from
my ear. I never had a chance to see one for so long a time. It was
lovely, and quite thrilling. The tiny thing filled the space with
the life vibration, it was all his.*

[Cock-crow : Chapter Twenty-six]

Few moments of the country year are as lovely as the green quiet
of an early summer morning. Rising today soon after sunrise, I
found a world as still as if the winds had not yet been created,
the whole summer landscape lying immersed in quiet as in a
dewy sea. Under the fresh sky and the increasing eastern light,
no branch or even leaf stirred on the old apples near the door;
not the smallest breath or whiplash of wandering air moved
within the grass bent over and sunken down as with a weight of
rain; in its hollow the pond was all one calm of peace and early
morning blue. Even the young swallows on the wires, sitting as
is their wont facing into the sun, kept their places and were still.

As I stood by the farm door looking down the hill slope into
this world so silent and at peace, I found myself beginning to
wonder about the country sounds which would presently arise
to break this blessedness of quiet. Nobody as yet seemed astir; I
could see no smoke as yet rising from the chimneys of the road.
Suddenly across the light and silence, across space and the immense peace of the morning, came a first morning sound, the
crow of a rooster from some farm beyond the fields. Clear and
challenging, and little muted by distance, it pierced the day—
that strange and threefold outcry at once musical and harsh
which is to my mind the symbol of the challenge of all things
living to life itself and its possible splendors and disasters. Danger, time, the shadow of the hawk, Death itself—in that cry all

were greeted and defied. And then next door I saw the smoke of a kitchen fire rising in blue unfoldings to the light.

Soon a cow lowed and another cow, breaking the quiet with that morning sound in which there is both recognition and a call for attention. Farm animals, horses in particular, are often sociable creatures, and make sociable noises and whinnyings which are greetings and little else. Half a mile down the road, my neighbor Irving Oliver's pair of white horses would now be showing a morning restlessness, and whinnying when they heard the kitchen door open and steps coming to the barn. From across the pond came the barking of a dog, but this sound was silenced almost at once, and the whole countryside returned again into its soundless peace.

The farm world, nevertheless, had begun its tasks. As I busied myself at some small chores of my own, I could see my neighbor Carroll Winchenbaugh coming and going about his barn. All up and down the country road the stoves had been lighted, the cows milked and the milk put away to cool, and breakfast made ready against the cares of the day. The hens, too, had been visited and fed, all in that strange sound of cackling and crooning from the flock, and neighbors would be carrying back the two or three eggs they had happened to see, leaving the real collection till later in the morning. The frisky, crafty eyed pig had had his "vittles," and the cats their saucer of milk beside the stove. These obligations seen to, the farm itself would presently be sitting down with a good conscience to its own repast.

The sun was rising into a sky of an even clearer blue; it promised to be a fine day. Soon one would hear the sounds of the manifold and unending work of the farm world, the sound of a farm truck, perhaps, or the noise of someone repairing and car-

109

pentering or the fine sound of a whetstone and a scythe. There would be voices in the distance across the fields, and it was almost time for the early morning train. Quiet as it remained, the day itself was coming to a new life. The heavy dew was going off into space, the pond had lost its quiescence of calm though it remained in morning peace, and a first wandering breeze, a mere sigh of the awakening air, presently fluttered the leaves of one branch of the older apple tree. The country day had begun.

⊰§ With sundown tonight there will begin one of the great festivals of the agricultural and solar year. It is June twenty-third, the night our era calls St. John's Eve, but which an earlier time dedicated to the triumph of fire and the sun. In the old Europe which inherited from the Bronze Age, this great feast of the Solstice was celebrated with multitudinous small fires lit throughout the countryside. Fire and the great living sun—perhaps it would be well to honor again these two great aspects of the flame. It might help us to remember the meaning of fire before the hands and fire as a symbol. As never before, our world needs warmth in its cold, metallic heart, warmth to go on and face what has been made of human life, warmth to remain humane and kind.

[To David McCord]

I look from the window to green New England fields, a blue pond, and a rocky pasture. My heart expands, and I make a special point each clear night of saluting the North Star. We each of us take up life again; again I mingle the pen and the plough, and at the moment the lovely fields are being mowed by a lanky neighbor mounted on a fearsome tractor huge as some specimen from a mechanical circus. We exist in a hay fragrance, a sort of "Jockey Club" of the earth, and at night the odor, subtly touched with some quality of the night, drifts inward through the screens.

* * *

The man who cuts our hay is a lank, black-haired, seventeenth-century creature; he doesn't belong to these Truman years. Apparently, he's quite tireless, and though he has a whole park of giant agricultural machines, he's always busy at something whenever you see him; no horse-and-plough farmer could be more constantly occupied. The night before last, he turned up here at 11:30 P.M. with the huge flat truck on which he loads his baled hay. Down into the fields he went, driving his truck among the hay bales scattered over the empty moonlit fields, and till 2 in the morning I saw him on these shorn slopes, working without a moment's pause under a gigantic full moon. It was strange to see that solitary figure down the field, often in silhouette against the moonlit pond, the immense peace of the country night around him. Yes, "seventeenth-century" is the adjective.

[Fog : Chapter Twenty-eight]

The day is warm and the skies genial, but I have a notion that a fog bank lies just off the coast and that we shall hear from it before the long afternoon has darkened to its close. The wind which moves across this earth of fluttering and innumerable leaves is the wind which stirs when fog is near, a restless, fidgety wind which is never still in the trees, and in the sky combs out the clouds like hair. And I know the meaning of that pale and milky bank of coastal haze which lies to seaward above our country scenes of woods and fields. As soon as the earth, losing its noonday heat, grows cool with the sun descending, the fog

111

will be upon us, taking over these blue summer skies just inland from the sea.

Even as I write, the vapor begins its slow and almost tidal advance from the horizon. The milky haze darkens and becomes a mystery of fog grey, and presently sailing fragments of the vapor are to be discovered drifting inland. The wind has not yet changed on the surface of the earth, it is still the restless south-west which is at play among the leaves and in the fruiting grass. But the southeasterly turn is coming, a breath of grey vapor, coolness, and the sea are coming towards us across the pond, coming not as a force, perhaps, but as a first physical sensation. The flying vapor is high, for the warm earth has still something to say and is lifting the wraiths into the higher air.

More arrive, and they now float between us and the earth's own cloud-forms in the higher blue. Presently it is more than the vanguard which is on the move; the whole sky of the eastern horizon is following after, advancing with the vast motion of the sea across some coastal plain of sand. Yet it is not a sky which is all one mass and substance of coolness and sea-grey; it has its lower fragments, its broken vapors, and its heavy, inexorable solemnities. Already the light is changing. The east has grown grey-dark, though the earth warmth and the late afternoon sun rule tranquilly in the open west above the wall of pines.

Farmerwise, we worry about our neighbor's hay. It lies in windrows on the carpet of the shorn field, windrow upon wind-row lying mounded and parallel like waves reaching the shore. The field is darkening under the darkening sky, the light upon it streaming level from the west. The neighbors, too, are apprehensive, for such an incoming of fog can mean a rainy day to follow. But help is at hand, for across our own wide field I can see the tanned figures of Carroll and his sons-in-law, Freddy French and Rupert Stevens, filling the big truck: indeed, I think

I see both Willa and Elaine pitching up great forkfuls beside their men. It is done; I hear the engine start, and a first fine load is on its way to the barn.

Meanwhile it is growing greyer and more cold. The incoming fog, moreover, is sinking as the earth chills, and I can now see a wisp of vapor between me and the pines across the road. The light grows silvery; the vapor has reached the western heavens, and is dimming and veiling over the great shield of the sun. A kind of hush seems to follow. The North Atlantic has the coast.

◄§ One of the greater mischiefs which confront us today is the growing debasement of the language. Our speech is a mere shadow of its incomparable richness, having on the one hand become vulgarized and on the other corrupted with a particularly odious academic jargon. Now, this is dangerous. A civilization which loses its power over its own language has lost its power over the instrument by which it thinks. Without some power over language there is neither greatness nor accuracy of thought. I am sure that this wasting disease of our English speech is one of the causes of today's bewilderment.

[To Dr. Neff]

In our good, native fashion all Maine is working in the hayfields without a shirt, making a sort of Yankee-cum-Abenaki golden age. I have always liked physical man held up against Nature, and busy at the work of man and Nature. All our various Christian religions are altogether too much out of relation to the living year—they inhabit a sort of ethical vacuum removed from the norm of natural experience. I'm all for Harvest festivals and things of that kind. They are both emotionally and religiously right.

113

[*To David McCord*]

There has been a run of lamprey eels up the Sheepscot, and a strange sight it was to see those rather gruesome, nightmare creatures fling themselves in a furious, writhing leap some six and eight feet into the sunlit air from the white water at the foot of a dam. It was really a spectacle out of some primitive mythology. It was indeed the "non-human" side of Nature.

[Fireflies : Chapter Twenty-nine]

We have had our first really blazing day. The sky poured down heat; the smell of hot soil rose from the cart tracks and the very fields, and wherever one looked from the farm, a blue heat-haze lay heavy on the earth. The ice truck arrived in a billow of dust and in another departed, leaving its fragmentary diamonds of chopped ice to melt to a cold dew on the grass beyond the shed. Coming to its own in the heat, our short-lived insect world made holiday, the nagging flies energized to new life and fierceness as they pestered us working in the fields.

So hot was the day that even the night was warm, and I slept with a second window open close beside my bed. Our nights, no matter what the day has been or what the set of the wind, are almost invariably cool or even autumnal cold. But this night was pleasant and warm; summer remained in our country world, brooding over field and granite ledge, over furrow holding the day's heat, and the beginning rows of northern corn.

Beyond the house and its quiet, there was only a vague world to be seen, a nocturnal world not of lines but of masses and vague shapes. Because there was no wind, not even a sigh to stir a dangling leaf, these earth masses were seemingly as without motion as a stone, the trees by the farm gate being but a solidity of darkness standing in its own dark. Yet was this world not without space. The stars were out, standing clearest overhead, and dimming as they moved low along the horizon above the other and more somber night of earth. Nor were great Antares and the stars of the zodiacal Scorpion the only lights to be seen. It was the wonder of the night below that it had its own stars.

Over the darkness and within it moved the fireflies. The field to the south was twinkling with their lights, and to the west, between the sleeping farm and the loom of the pines, the tiny, golden-phosphorescent brilliances glowed in the dark, moving in numbers over the gloom that was the field. It was not quite a dance, this pulsation and rhythm that was at once everywhere and nowhere, neither was it mechanical, being so full of mystery and waywardness.

What a beautiful light it was, I thought, as I watched the glow of some one insect, pulsating on a rising flight, pass close by and against the dark of an old High Top apple tree. It had something of moonlight to it, and something of lightning, and something of the suddenness of lightning. I am told that in certain tropical countries a field of fireflies appears to pulsate and glow in one simultaneous and inexplicable rhythm, but I have never seen such a phenomenon here, and prefer the broken and spontaneous twinkling of our own midsummer nights.

The "firefly" or "lightning bug" is a small beetle, a brownish and inoffensive creature. The light and its flashing are supposed to have something to do with the mating season. This may be so. On the other hand, the light and its flashing may simply be another example of the creative splendor and whimsicality— there is no other word—of the mystery of nature and the earth.

⚜ I return to the word "whimsicality" which I used to describe one of the characteristics of Nature. Without some recognition of that element, we do not correctly weigh our visible world. In the Kingdom of Life, Nature sometimes works with a clear purpose of adaptation, constructing, for instance, those wonderful creatures, the leaf-imitating butterflies, and those living twigs, the "walking sticks." On the other side of this assumption and evidence of purpose, there exists a whole creation of pure fantasy having no explicable relation whatever between purpose and design. You see birds in the tropics that are living paint-boxes, at once exquisitely beautiful and wildly absurd. When naturalists get too serious, I like to think of this side of Nature, so creative, imaginative, and full of gusto, and of the fantastic creatures which are its jocund gift.

[Auction : Chapter Thirty]

"I have here a small pitcher with blue and yellow flowers. How much am I offered? Fifty. Who'll make it seventy-five? Seventy-five, who'll make it a dollar? A dollar: who'll make it a dollar and a quarter? A dollar and a quarter I have: who'll make it a dollar-fifty? Anybody make it a dollar-fifty? Any bids? Sold to the lady in the brown hat for a dollar and a quarter."

It is the very perfection of a summer's day, and on a side street of the seacoast town and on the lawn of an old white house, a whole miscellany of household goods stands in the open air under two venerable elms. There are old benches covered with kitchen china and table china, a parlor organ, chairs of all kinds, some arranged in rows, boxes of old books, pictures stacked dustily, their backs to the observer, wooden bowls and eggbeaters, and spool beds and horsehide trunks.

Auctions are a part of our adventure of the summer. We all go to them when they are held near by, especially if we knew the family whose things are being auctioned off. We buy agricultural tools and implements at farm auctions, and at town auctions are liable to bid for what takes our fancy. Because we are an old, a

116

conservative, and a thrifty people, and shipbuilders and sea-farers withal, there is no telling here what an auction may bring to light. I have seen a small cottage on the coast produce a superbly carved ceremonial comb from the old Bight of Benin, and as for grandfathers' clocks, they used to take them home in hayracks, carefully laid flat on a cushion of new hay.

The weather being so fine, and the auction so well advertised, a sizable number of townspeople and summer people have gathered in the driveway and on the lawn. There is also a figure I have never known to be absent from any auction anywhere—somebody's black-and-tan hound dog seated not on his sitdown, but on the small of his back, and trying perseveringly to scratch the bottom of his chin.

People are coming, people are going, small boys are moving about, the usual antique dealers are turning plates over, and buyers are carrying various purchases off to their parked cars. Going about in the throng, our summer people enliven the entire scene with modern color and gaiety. "How much am I offered?" "No, Ma'am, I wouldn't say it was an antique." "Don't know what you'd call this— " Pause, and an answer from many ladies replying antiphonally, "It's a tea-tray." A spirited battle takes place over a "Boston rocker" painted black and gold with an oriental bird in golden scrollwork on the headboard.

In terms of town and village history, I know well what I am seeing. It is not only the last of some old household which is being scattered to the wolves, but the lares and penates of America's early nineteenth century. This "omnium gatherum" of furniture is our 1840's and 1850's with the usual few—and bad—additions from the 1870's plus something of the flowery-bowery world of the bouncing early 1900's. Browsing among the pictures, I find that old-time favorite, "A Yard of Kittens," and behind it a particularly good late eighteenth-century portrait-engraving of President George Washington seated in his Presidential chair.

"I think you'll like what he's putting up now," says Elizabeth quickly. "Let's go closer."

"I now show you— " begins the auctioneer, and not only do I like what he holds up to view but I feel that it would take a charge of bears to separate me from it. It is a painting, a "genuine oil painting," about twenty inches square and framed in a gay but not too gaudy gilt frame of the late Eighties or the Nineties.

Now, pictures are my weakness, and this is a prize. Done by some rustic and inspired amateur about fifty or sixty years ago, it depicts in fine, bold color a scene full of dramatic action and bravura, the departure of a horse-drawn fire engine from the enginehouse. The back of the picture is the enginehouse archway full of golden light, and the foreground is the engine itself pouring out a long tress of wonderful smoke while two gigantic dapple-grey horses plunge forward in an artistic moment of outstretched necks and lashing hoofs. They are neither real horses nor rocking horses, but a combination of the two such as only a genius could achieve. A fireman in blue with handlebar moustaches leans forward to drive, and a second figure leans out from the firebox.

"Sold to Mr. Beston for three dollars and fifty cents!"

We have hung it in the winter kitchen beside the fireplace, and the horses have been promptly christened "Major" and "Prince."

⋅§ The other day, while looking at an album of good modern photographs of ancient Greek portrayals of the old classical life, many of them entirely "realistic," I found myself wondering what the quality was in these ancient faces which is absent from ours. The modern face is a tired one, but it was not the absence of fatigue which interested me in these countenances of the past. They too must have known their times of weariness. What was it? Assurance? Acceptance? A sense of roots in an objective world?

I give no answer to my own question. Of one thing, however, I am sure: these people did not ask too much. Perhaps asking too much is an error more dangerous than we realize, a thing of strong poison to the human soul. Our world would do well for a while to muse upon the serenity and happiness possible within our human and earthly limitations.

[From Chapter Thirty-one]

᪄ One of the complications of the problem of the machine is the fact that just as certain people are born hunters and farmers, others are born machinists. The mechanical strain is in humanity, and if it has given us a machine civilization increasingly difficult to manage, it has also given us the wheel and the knife. I do not forget that memorable saying of my old friend Edward Gilchrist that "the secret of the artificer is the secret of civilization." Yet what we must ask today is whether or not the mechanist strain has increased out of all bounds, and taken over an undue proportion of the way of life. It is well to use the wheel but it is fatal to be bound to it.

[To David McCord]

The other night, happening to have read late, I turned out my bedside lamp to see that the sky beyond and through the apple trees was all a glory of starlight and brightest stars, and hastening

*into a robe and slippers went out of doors to see if Jupiter would
not presently appear above the darkened earth-line and the vast
melancholy of the woods. Yes, there it was, seemingly just
having cleared the horizon of hills, a portent and a splendor of
purest golden light, even of that "light" the Gnostics, like St.
John, made theological and opposed to the nothingness and
abysm of the dark. There was not a sound to be heard in our
earth world of the farms, and across the pond, all the houses had
gone quietly to bed. Sometimes, at such an hour, I hear a loon
call in the distance, but this night there came no sound at all.*

[From Chapter Thirty-two]

&§ This is not a wheat country though we can grow it here;
our fields are fields of corn. Beautiful as such a field may be when
the corn is standing high and the great harsh leaves stir with their
grating sound in the hot August wind, it is often of the wheat
that I think, of the ancient plant which is the token and symbol
of man and of order and civilization, of the wheat of Egypt and
the threshing floors, of the bright mornings of the harvest and the
golden, burning afternoons, and of the last sheaf brought home
in rustic triumph from the fields.

We have a tradition which is carried on by thoughts and
words: has it been remarked that tradition is also carried on by
things? Wheat itself is tradition, and good bread is tradition;
not without reason have the great religions honored the breaking
of bread together. Perhaps it would be well for us to recognize
this body of tradition which lies in things and be more aware of
it. We have grown blind to it and forget that apart from words it
binds human being to human being, and that a way of life must
seek to preserve the strengths whose roots go deep.

[*To Dr. Neff*]

We've been away on a week-end to the Indian Reservation at Old Town. Sometime last fall they dug into a "Red Paint" cemetery while putting through or improving an island road, and I've always wanted to possess a Red Paint artifact—to use the rather grim word of the archaeologists. So to Old Town we went, and I wangled-purchased a fishline sinker or lure, more or less shell-shaped, for Betsy B., and the Indian threw in a beautiful green-slate knife or axe blade. The Red Paint culture is the unknown, very, very ancient prehistoric culture which preceded our present Algonquin occupation, disappearing thousands of years ago, no one knowing where it went or what happened to it. They made exceptionally beautiful cutting tools, but did not know the use of the bow and arrow.

[From Chapter Thirty-three]

Has it occurred to anyone that as civilization has become more urbanized and city populations greater than those who live by agriculture, there has been a parallel increase in war and violence? Apparently some relation exists which is not entirely economic. The farmer would reply that agriculture is an art of peace which requires a peaceful time, and that agricultural populations, as seen in history, are not by nature aggressively military. A population of planters and farmers, moreover, cannot leave its crops to shift for themselves and gather themselves together into barns. The machine, on the contrary, can be left to shift for itself. This does not improve it, but it can be deserted on its concrete floor. Above all, the machine world is barren of that sense of responsibility which is the distinguishing spiritual mark and heritage of the long ownership of land. I think history would agree that though spears may be beaten into pruning hooks, pruning hooks are less frequently beaten into spears.

[Union Fair : Chapter Thirty-five]

The side road leaves U.S. Route 1 at the top of a wooded hill. For a few level miles it leads on through a ragged farming country, then climbing a steep knoll, presently opens on a great and widening view of mountains, a blue pond, and an agricultural landscape set about with thriving farms. At one end of the pond is a pleasant old-fashioned village in its elms, and about a mile beyond, its location marked by rows of parked autos massed in a trodden field, is the Fair. It is only a small fair but it is our fair, and already the distant squeal of mechanical music floats to us across the green meadows and the rural scene.

The farm family has long had a warm place in its heart for the fair at Union Village. Our smaller fairs have been one of the casualties of the war, either ceasing to be or dragging on a poor existence as horse races tied to shabby carnivals, but the Union Fair has kept its popularity and retained its standing as a genuine old-style agricultural show. It has its horses and its cattle, its great yokes of oxen and its bulls with nose rings and blue ribbons, its handicrafts and quilts and jars of vegetables, its horse races and its contests, its gypsy fortune-tellers, and its giant swings.

Well, let's go in. "This way, please. Easy now. OK." A pleasant, well-mannered Boy Scout with various Scout badges and a very grown-up and professional police badge, shows us where to park; the doors slam, and away to the fair we go.

Almost at once there is something fine to see. The great teams of farm horses which are going to enter the pulling contests are coming down the field from their quarters with each owner standing on the stoneboat dragged behind, and holding the reins with the look and assurance of a Roman charioteer in overalls. The brass harness studs and buckles shine like brazen gold in the beautiful morning light; gaudy plumes bob on the huge heads, and the brushed tails have the grace of waterfalls. A fine pair of strawberry roans takes my eyes as down the slope they go to the little grandstand and the dragging area.

"Hello, George. Showing here?" "Yes, got a first prize yesterday for the Guernsey bull." "Hello, Randall, I suppose you've brought your steers?" "Yes, going in this afternoon. The kid here got second yesterday with his yoke." Yellow-haired Ordway, aged nine, grins shyly. "Ordway, you show Mr. and Mrs. Beston your red ribbon."

The oxen are all of them in their shed. There are many yokes, for the country around Union is one of the last regions of the republic to rear and use these great Virgilian beasts. They handle better than horses when our winter comes with its deeps and drifts of snow. Going to the pulling contests for oxen, we see the real thing in drivers, a country boy about fifteen years old who looks as if he came from some small farm. When his steers pull, he throws, as it were, his will in with theirs, and placing his hand on the flank of the nigh ox, drives forward not only with his urging voice and his eagerness but also with his leaning body —the boy and his great creatures all in one rhythm of work and rustic ambition.

It is interesting to watch, and I am glad when he carries off a prize.

Such a medley of impressions force themselves all at once on the senses that it is hard not to be a bit confused when strolling about in the heart of the fair. The smell of popcorn and the din of loudspeakers. Other smells of coffee urns and frying hamburgers. The rustic smell of farm animals, and the smell of trodden grass and earth.

On the midway, I see some gypsy women with beaded purses at their hips, standing by the entrances to their fortune-telling booths. I always wish them a polite "good-day" in Romany, a friend once having taught me certain greeting words. The stunt at first silences them with an immense suspicion, and then they all laugh merrily and wickedly, and give Elizabeth and me special recognition when we pass. We have one gypsy word well established in the English language—our word "pal," which is the gypsy for comrade.

So sauntering about, we reach our car, and drive off full of plans for the next fair.

❧ Every once in a while, when one lives in the country and observes wild animals, one is sure to come upon dramas and acts of courage which profoundly stir the heart. The tiniest birds fight off the marauder, the mother squirrel returns to the tree already scorched by the oncoming fire; even the creatures in the pond face in their own strange fashion the odds and the dark. Surely courage is one of the foundations on which all life rests! I find it moving to reflect that to man has been given the power to show courage in so many worlds, and to honor it in the mind, the spirit, and the flesh.

[*To his wife*]

Looking from the window yesterday, I saw a man in a buggy driving towards us from the Rollinses', and behind the buggy a something that might have been a hitched-on cow which

124

presently became two cows. The enchanted princesses, having broken pasture, were being led back to their hill. The enchanted princesses, this year, are not really princesses at all. One, the Guernsey heifer, is clearly a palace attendant who got enchanted while the enchanting happened—and she's not so much an attendant as an estimable local lady who came on Wednesdays to mark the linen with the Cnossos arms—a sort of Minoan Miss Lincoln—and she knows quite well who she is and doesn't like it at all! Her companion is a Cnossos schoolgirl with a pug nose (a Jersey) who happened to be passing the palace on the way home from the afternoon session, and though she has accepted it all as children accept things, she has an instinctive feeling that all is not as it might be. The old red horse pulled, and the ladies, with twisted rebellious heads and horns awry, went down the lane to the rocks and junipers.

[To David McCord]

In my attic I cherish a special shelf of country material. Were I younger, I think I'd write an entertaining and "Dionysian" treatise on witchcraft and agriculture which would include a way-map of the routes to the nearest covens together with a page on favorite dance steps and tunes—a sort of witches' "vade mecum" for the use of travelers in Britain. There are many folk-memories here of the Nobleboro witch who flourished circa 1840–1860. A fine old creature, and had she been living today, we would not be plagued with these almost annual summer drouths. Why didn't those idiot persecutors see that one of the most valuable members of a community is that member with a power over nature?

125

[The Fishermen : Chapter Thirty-six]

Every time I go shopping to Damariscotta, and especially on Saturday afternoons, I meet the fishermen on the street or in the stores, bronzed and sunburnt as the sea does the weathering, and marked by the folded-over rubber boots which are the sign of the craft. I come upon them now buying groceries, now buying marine hardware and coils of new line, now reading the morning paper and waiting their turn in the barber's chair. Because it is cool, even cold, at sea, they wear their flannel shirts and woolen pants through the year, sewing bold patches everywhere when the old cloth wears through.

I call them fishermen, but the term and the rubber boots loosely include the run of our people who live by the sea. There are true fishermen among them with their own boats; there are clammers whom the state authorities are forever checking; there are lobstermen with their boats and lobster traps; there are diggers of the seaworms which are used for bait—this last is now among us a very profitable trade. Whatever they may chance to be, and whether boat-owners or clammers, one great influence binds them all together: they are people of the sea. Fiercely independent, courageous, and, according to some, jestingly truculent when in the mood, they drive to town in their old cars from their coves and villages, and will have nothing but the best when they buy.

Herring from the weirs are now selling for over fifteen dollars a barrel at the wharf, and lobsters are high and the late summer catch a good one, but it is not prices that hold these neighbors to their craft. Not for them are the hayfork, the plough, and the barn shovel, but the bait tub, the salt box, and the barbed hook; not for such as these the rooted fields, but the more perilous and unquiet pastures of the blue. Before the automobile

126

opened up the coast the fishing villages were isolated and apart, a situation reflected in the character of the towns. The last fisherman to wear an earplug of gold—an inheritance from Elizabethan England—was an old-timer at Monhegan Island, and it is not very long ago since he gave up forever his sheath knife and the sea.

Your true fishermen with their own boats and gear are the natural leaders and nobility of the craft. Today most of them are young or youngish men, for the old fisherman—as a figure—largely vanished with the great days of sail. Nowadays, moreover, a man with a boat has to be a competent engineer; his life depends upon it. Many of our sea folk, too, are light-haired, and this I take to be a reflection of the Scandinavian blood in the British strain which first colonized these coves and isles.

Because I am living on fresh water and on a farm, these are not my people, though I stretch out a hand to them for I am seacoast born and bred. But I know something of the life which they carry on in our cold and brilliant waters with the great mountain-shaped hills rising blue against the lonely inland sky. I know the lonely coves in the spruce-clad coast line, and the rocks over which the rising tide breaks in a crystalline smother of tumbling and rolling foam. And the bitter seas of winter, too, are theirs, with the driving vapors of icy days drifting low above the waves and hiding the foundation of the islands behind their scarves of mist.

A hardy folk. If our doctrinaires have put upon men's shoulders more than they can or are willing to carry, and we pass into some slavery to a cannibal form of the state, these sea folk will be the last to wear the tattooed mark. It will not be easy to overcome the heritage of the other disciplines and freedoms of the sea. So I like to see the sheath knives and the rubber boots and the patches and the direct eyes. They are something to hold on to in any nation.

⮕ As I watch the fire burning in the great fireplace on a first chilly night, I do not wonder that fire and the mystery of fire have played so important a part in the great religions of mankind. The power to kindle that ever-hungry flame must have been the first great achievement of man on his way to fuller being; with fire he both metaphorically and in all reality could see ahead in to the dark. "Fire is a good servant but a bad master." So runs the proverb. I can remember hearing it said in the long ago. To me, it is the element which is always a part of the mystery and beauty of the world. The earth may be shabbily and wickedly broken, the river and the air befouled, but the living flame, rising from whatever source, is beauty from its first appearance and as beauty lives. There is no compromise with flame, and not without reason has it served us as a symbol of that unknown to whose ultimate mystery we can but lift our uncertain hands.

[From Chapter Thirty-seven]

⮕ I understand from various friends that there is a campaign going on in rural areas to re-open our old-fashioned, one-room country schools. Well—one might go farther and fare worse. What such schools used to be able to give us is something we very badly need, and that is a real first sense of being a member of a definite community. Without more of that sense than we now have, there is not much sensible hope of the better nation out of which must come the better world. The big, overcrowded modern schools with their parades and drum-majorettes and courses in "citizenship" just do not give this vital sense of human association. I shall watch any such small school experiment with interest, and so here's a Porter apple for dear teacher, and may the children be sent home early when the afternoon darkens and the stove glows red, and the snow begins to fall.

[From Chapter Thirty-nine]

❧ When I am here by myself, and the small dog and I share together the too-quiet evening and the open fire, I read the agricultural papers and journals which have been put aside in the kitchen cupboard for just such a solitary night. I never read through such a basketful without being struck by the good, sound, honest English of the writing, by the directness and simplicity of the narratives, and by the skill and forthright vigor of the arguments. Whether the topic be tomatoes or tenpenny nails, their writers know how to say things and say them well.

I am glad that the country world thus retains a power to use our English tongue. It is part of its sense of reality, of its vocabulary of definite terms, and of its habit of earthly common sense. I find this country writing an excellent corrective of the urban vocabulary of abstractions and of the emotion disguised as thinking which abstractions and humbug have loosed upon the world. May there always be such things as a door, a milk pail, and a loaf of bread, and words to do them honor.

[*To his mother-in-law*]

We are having a lovely, sunlit, golden fall, an autumn so beautiful that the farmers hereabouts are beginning to look askance at the blue skies and to wish for rain. Old-fashioned farm folk here use the word "fountain" in its Biblical sense—the only region that I know of where such a usage continues—and they say "the wells are pretty low, but the fountains have held up well this year." Every time I hear it, I think of passages in the King James and of "the fountains of the great deep" being opened.

When cold weather came, I used to bring the cook-stove into the fireplace kitchen, but that arrangement heats the room up like a boiler factory when the outside temperature warms up. I am this year going to leave the cooking range just where it is, in the little kitchen, and make that kitchen as snug as I can. It goes below freezing every night, but nobody minds it at all, and the children, bless 'em, look especially well. Last night, it went down to 27. Whenever it's cool in the bigger kitchen, I build a fire in the fireplace, and make it fine and cozy. And Betsy has a fire in her room all day long, a big log for the night, and a fine, warm, old-fashioned feather bed to sleep on. The children's rooms are comfortable on the coldest nights, and they have a stove to dress by, and eat their meals in the warm, cozy fireplace kitchen.

[To his sister-in-law]

The water in our great well-spring is now below the intake. As the weather continues warm, we are able to use the pond supply, but at the most, I doubt if I can continue this beyond a fortnight. (You can use outdoor pipes here after October 15 to 20 only if you make up your bed beside the pipe and have your plumbing wrenches under the pillow ready to drain everything.) So if the cold weather makes a jump and the autumnal rains fail to come, we shall be carrying water like 80 percent of the people of the state.

The air is full of the smoke of the wood fires. Yesterday at noon, it was so thick over East Neck that you could hardly see down to the Olivers'. There are now some sixty-four fires burning in the state, and there is still no sign of any rain. It is quite

*terrifying to look up and see a vast pale column of smoke rising
from the woods towards this lovely, quite irresponsible blue.
By some curious alchemy, the smoke, once it gets into the
house, has quite a different odor from what it has outdoors—
more pungent, more acrid and woodsy.*

[North to The Forks: Chapter Forty-one]

The blue Kennebec lay below us to the west, its rushing waters
rippled with the sunlight of a bright October morning, and to
the east above us on hills and mountains, the forest blazed in its
autumnal coat of many colors. Along these waters and through
this same wilderness, I remembered, Arnold had made his way
to Quebec at the beginning of the Revolution; over these very
rapids his men had dragged their clumsy and heavily loaded
bateaux; on these very slopes they had built their evening fires.
In their village homespuns and cowhide boots, in their torn
woolen stockings and woolen scarves, the figures of the expedition
peopled the scene again in my mind's eye as I drove north, they,
too, facing north in another splendor of autumn one hundred
and seventy-one long years ago.

Uninhabited and for the most part uninhabitable, the forest
still covers the lonely country of "the height of land" and the
immense region of the boundary mountains. For well over a
century lumber companies have used these hundreds of wilderness miles, and everywhere are old tote-roads leading to nowhere,
their corduroy lengths and swamp crossings long ago sunk and
rotted into the black forest mire. These last years bears have
made it particularly their own, and a friend tells me that they
are now so numerous that at the lumber camps their prowling
visits alarm newcomers from the French villages over the border.

And what shall one say of presences much more mysterious
than bears? One of the "undeveloped townships" of the woods—

131

or as we call them here, "plantations"—has from time immemorial borne the curious and lovely name of "The Enchanted."
People may say to you of a neighbor, "He's gone hunting in
The Enchanted." Fifty years ago in this plantation a wood
voice, a seemingly human voice, sent a whole lumber camp out
searching in the night, yet in the morning there were no strange
footsteps in the snow. Well—a Canada lynx can make very
curious noises, but the old woodsmen always spoke of the sound
they heard as "the voice," and the incident is remembered to
this day.

With the cutting of so much spruce and pine, the forest is
surely more of a hardwood region than it was in Arnold's day.
On the tote-roads the pale and papery beech leaves now strew
the forest clearings together with the deep scarlet of the maples
and the beautiful tan-bronze of the fronded ash. Even so, the
dark of the returning evergreens is to be seen on every side, young
pines, spruces, and fir balsams rising up in power from the floors
of fallen leaves. On the highways, too, pass thundering trucks
piled with pine logs so giant that one wonders in what lost,
hidden valley they were found.

At the village of The Forks, the expedition left the Kennebec
and followed Dead River to the "Chain of Ponds" and the ragged,
desolate, and stunted "height of land." What lumber there was
seems to have been long ago appropriated, and vast fires have
reduced the region to a wilderness of bush, bouldery mires, and
alder-bordered ponds; much of it is now owned by a hunting and
fishing club. I have had old woodsmen tell me that in one of the
ponds lies some waterlogged planking which some imagine is
part of one of Arnold's bateaux.

I know the region, but last week I did not go beyond The
Forks. The village today is but a line of rather frontierish houses
built to the west of the confluence beyond an old-fashioned iron

132

bridge painted an old-fashioned and faded red. The tourist season being about over, few cars overtook us driving on to Canada by the black road which crosses the boundary a good thirty miles east of Arnold's narrow ponds in their archaic gully in the bush.

The old general store at The Forks, I noticed, stood closed and empty, though its black-and-gold sign was still fixed to the wall. There was something on it about fishing tackle, groceries, and cigars. A kind of porch stood before the door and the empty windows, and we sat down there awhile to rest ourselves from driving and listen to the murmur of the Kennebec below the bridge. The sounds of rivers can bemuse the mind, and I am sure that if I had but waited longer, I might have heard the far-off shouts of Arnold's men and the last of the talk and the voices as the expedition moved up the Dead River to the woods.

৵ Every autumn I watch for one great star. It is the star Capella, and when in September I look to the north and see it rising over the somber roof-line of a deserted barn, I know that winter is near. Night after night it stands a little higher above the earth when twilight comes, and when arrives the true cold and the dark, it has cleared the floors of earth and the low mists and is rising on its great arc into that northeast whence come the birds whose clamor sometimes wakes us in the earlier night. There is an order established against whose laws only fools will struggle, an order whose acceptance is the very cornerstone of life and peace.

[To David McCord]

We have just had an afternoon and early night of rain from a morning's sky of Hebridean mist, a welcome intermittency of

133

showers, for our wells have all been retreating down their hollow
pillars of fieldstone and moss, much troubling householders and
small frogs. After supper Betsy and I went to the "attic chamber"
(the whole, ancient, raftered top of the lesser house), brought
up the pleasant, golden lamp, lit a small fire, and talked and
listened to the rain, "the small crepitation of the rain," as I
once wrote, and forgive me a quotation from myself. What a
lovely sound it is! Now gathering to a drumming roar, now
dissolving, now diminuendo to a milder sound, now ceasing
altogether to begin, crepitando, with drops which have just
outdistanced the others. The attic is full of books bought at
country auctions, old bound magazines of the '90's, illustrated
compendiums of the Civil War, collections of "Wit and Humor,
English and American," and omnium gatherums of Famous
Events and so on, all surprisingly good reading and amusing to
look through. So we passed a pleasant country evening, and
later on I popped a bowl of popcorn and brought it up to our
retreat, sinfully good and buttery.

   While I was writing the very first sentence of this letter, I
heard an odd, faint sound, and looking out saw a flock of a
thousand or so chattering blackbirds sweep across the field
and the roof of my little house; and what pleased me most, I
think, was the sight of the vivid scatter of shadows cast by the
last of the birds and seen from the window after the army had
crossed my roof and gone in one queer wild sound down to the
lake. These gothic migrations of blackbirds are a feature of our
October. I see such a "peuplade" (there is no good English
word) in the river fields nearer the open ocean. The sound they
make is entirely different from the starling gabble, "that species
of bird Yiddish," as Hudson exactly and evilly said; these natives
make a dry shrill sound, and the gathering flies with a kind of
close-knit directness, disdaining the starlings' vast and really
quite beautiful evolutions.

134

[Early Morning: Chapter Forty-three]

There is a time in the later autumn when a vast cloud of fog forms every night above the pond, and, rising to fill the vale of the enclosing shores, spills over and out upon higher land as from a bowl filled and overflowing. No longer a vaporous mist but a mass thickened and opaque, it lies so dense at sunrise that sometimes I can scarce see from the farm to the farm gate, and I walk to whatever chores await me through a world without known bounds and suspended at once in morning silence and humid nothingness. Farmers, however, are early risers, and fog is a good carrier of sound, and presently I am sure to hear far noises across the texture of mist and perhaps the distant challenge of some farmyard chanticleer.

Thick as the fog lies floating on the earth, there is usually a blue sky standing open overhead. By ten o'clock, on any sunshiny morning, we commonly have our world again. The mist dissolves rather than lifts, and as it thins, the pasture fence and the golden trees appear, and the slow transformation scene ends with a view of the other side of the pond and its shores of pines scattered through with hardwoods in all their blazing color. Sometimes scarves and last wreaths of mist linger in the coldness of the shadowed woods, but the sun will have none of this, and presently these, too, melt and are gone, and the world belongs again to autumn and the blue and spacious day.

Halfway down the east slope, I could see my neighbors, the Olivers, gathering in their beans. The white horse, Prince, and the blue hayrack stood in the heart of the great field, and beyond the rack moved the figures of Father Oliver, his son Irving, and four-year-old grandson, John, in a red sweater, bright as any autumnal leaf. The beans had been stacked on stout poles, as is our local custom, and from the house I could see Irving taking

135

up, one after another, these brown and withered towers, first swaying the poles about and working them loose in the earth. Both Elwell and Irving then laid their huge burdens in the rack with the poles slanting forward, and each pole, I thought, seemed taller than a man.

No more would I look down and see these rustic pillars scattered over the field in the cold autumnal moonlight; no more would I see the small migrants flying to and fro between the pole tops and the ground. The load assembled, Irving climbed into the rack and took up the reins. Father Oliver then handed in the little boy and climbed in himself. The white horse started, stopped, and started again, and the load of harvest life came slowly up the hill.

The old-fashioned "baked bean" is an important part of our farm economy in this higher north. With plenty of "baking beans" in storage, a piece of salt pork, and a jug of molasses in the "buttery," a wood range that knows its business in the kitchen, and a family beanpot in the oven, we feel ready here for anything that may arrive when the north and east darken beyond the hills and a three-day storm begins to howl.

�⋅§ How pleasant to spend some time with a singing family! During my own lifetime, one of the most dismal social changes of our world has been the disappearance of singing as part of human life and the work that has to be done. People used to sing, now you scarcely hear anyone even whistle. The world is poorer for the loss. There is nothing like music for giving one a sense of solidarity, and it lightens both labor and the heart.

[*To his wife*]

The air has cooled, the ground frozen again to some consistency if not firmness, a wind blows from a blue and clear and

milky-cold northwest, and the dead oak leaves flutter and twinkle
on one great tree. On Tuesday morning I saw something rather
fine. A whole migrating company of wildfowl, about a hundred
or so I should say, and "ducks" by species, came into our cove,
and well in to our shore, and remained there the whole morning.
The birds were "whistlers" for the most part, black and white
with a black head, but there were other species as well, a few
seagulls even, and I think two mature loons and three or four
immature ones. The company floated, closed in together
comfortably and sociably, bobbing black and white, dipping
down, standing up and fluttering their wings, and feeding. Vast
"murmurations" of starlings visit us, making a noise like a distant
automobile or a rumble of small thunder as they take off from
somewhere near the house.

Who shall band those fugitive birds?

[The Wild Geese Go Over : Chapter Forty-four]

So comes to an end as pleasant an October as any of us can remember, an October so mild and warm that it might have been
a second and more tranquil summer. Because there have been
few heavy rains it has been a fine season for field work and
harvesting, and on all the farms the autumn ploughing has been
unhurriedly done, the potatoes dug, the apples picked, the field
manured, and the house gardens raked clean of the pale and
sprawling ghosts which the heavier frosts left withering on the
ground. Now comes November and a colder sky with a prophecy
of winter in its lessened and russet light, and something of the
vast silence of winter in the air.

It is a time for rustic satisfaction, and a time, in the old phrase,
"to count one's blessings," be they golden Hubbards or a barrel
of farm cider, yet a touch of melancholy can steal its way into the

137

mood. The great, earthy, and out-of-door tasks of the farm are over and done, and on these cold nights when a rising wind rattles the windows and the ragged clouds sail across the moon, we know in our warm kitchens what will presently come down upon us from the solitudes of the north. Strengthened and provisioned like fortresses, our cordwood stacked under cover and our cellars filled, we should not fear the Northeaster and the wind running in above the sea.

Fortresses we are, fortresses of the life of man in the beauty and glare and sunshine of the snow. In Maine we call our preparation for the siege—and the phrase is ancestral—"housing-up." The women of the farms now put in order the rooms which will not be used, stripping the beds and folding up and laying away the blankets, placing chairs to one side, and carefully putting each thing that might be breakable into a bureau drawer. During the last of autumn, when such rooms are not too cold, these deserted chambers have a magnetic quality of attracting to their chilly emptiness all sorts of things which must be kept at a proper temperature, baskets of winter pears, for instance, and late-ripening apples, and even jars of jelly put aside to "set" awhile.

Today Elizabeth, together with our neighbor, Mrs. Ruth Erskine (who is pianist at our Grange), has been busy at this domestic ritual. Blankets have been hanging on the line all morning in this coldish light, the hooked rugs have been laid flat and swept on the grey veranda, and the company teacups taken from their shelf on the what-not in the parlor and put away, each wrapped in its bit of newspaper. The house retreats upon itself but its life is not weakened; it is merely given more unity and concentration.

It is the task of the men to see to the state of the house and barn, make repairs, and check on the primary supplies. If there is a coal stove in use part of the winter, the coal must be in; kerosene barrels filled, too, and the stovewood as far as possible got under cover. Today Ellis Simmons and I have been working outside. The screens have come off, some willingly, some obstinately, the storm doors and the double shutters fitted, two more cords of wood stacked, and the pond water-system drained and the great pump greased and laid up for winter.

A little after four o'clock a great wild sound in the sky sent us all rushing out of doors. A huge flock of Canada geese, flying unusually low, was passing by directly above the farm. Arriving from the east, the line swung south toward the local inlets and the sea, hovered for a few minutes in milling indecision, and disappeared, still apparently confused, into the cold and wintry light a little south of west.

❧ However various may be the tasks which man is given to attend to upon this earth, his major occupation is a concern with life. To accomplish this duty, he must honor life, even if he honors it but blindly, knowing that life has a sacredness and mystery which no destruction of the poetic spirit can diminish. The curtain has just rung down on a great show and carnival of death and the air is still poisoned and we are poisoned. Our strength and intelligence have been used to counter the very will and purpose of the earth. We had better begin considering not what our governments want but what the earth imposes.

[The End : Chapter Forty-six]

As the seasonal light decreases, and the arc of our northern sun becomes a mere geometric leftover of its midsummer sweep and exaltation, I watch the pond changing color from its autumnal blue to a kind of austere and silvery grey. Now that the water is becoming almost as cold as the air, the great fog bank which used to gather on frosty nights is to be seen no more, though once or twice, after a night of bitter cold, I have seen vague wisps and thin tatters of trailing mist clearing off as the sun rose to begin his short-lived day. The other morning all the slopes were covered with frost, and the residual mists floated up the sides of the hills, and dissolved on the higher land into nothingness and light.

I have long had the notion that our northern ponds were at their bluest about a fortnight after the Vernal and, later, the Autumnal Equinox. The blue of early April, moreover, has always seemed to me brighter and more living than the colder and more severe blue of the clearer October air. In the full solar splendor of midsummer there is too much light in the sky to give us the blue of water at its best, and the pleasant, varied tones of summer are paler tones of the air and the mystery overhead. Now there has come a second paling and a second withdrawal, and though there is blue to be seen on the water, it is a blue which is near to silver and to steel.

A force of nature itself, the pond awaits the deeper cold and its own emergence from some first and iron night floored with a first darkness and motionlessness of ice. The trees of the shore are skeletons of winter, the grasses and sedges of the little beach have withered to spears of straw and russet brown, and on the tiny crescent of cold sand a submerged garland of matted oak leaves checks the ripples blown ahead of a morning wind which has risen with the sun.

So draws to a close the country year. It is late at night, and musing here alone in the kitchen of the farm, my papers and pencils spread about on the table under the peaceful light, I venture to set down a statement of a countryman's unchanged belief. What has come over our age is an alienation from Nature unexampled in human history. It has cost us our sense of reality and all but cost us our humanity. With the passing of a relation to Nature worthy both of Nature and the human spirit, with the slow burning down of the poetic sense together with the noble sense of religious reverence to which it is allied, man has almost ceased to be man. Torn from earth and unaware, having neither the inheritance and awareness of man nor the other sureness and integrity of the animal, we have become vagrants in space, desperate for the meaninglessness which has closed about us. True humanity is no inherent and abstract right, but an achievement, and only through the fullness of human experience may we be as one with all who have been and all who are yet to be, sharers and brethren and partakers of the mystery of living, reaching to the full of human peace and the full of human joy.

[To his wife]

Things I thought you might like:

The old man who used to be a figurehead carver. He made all the figureheads around here. They are quite poor, now, and old, and his sister peddles cottage cheese through the village.

The last survivors of the old sailing ship era here were not people but parrots. When Jake was a boy, the town was full of old parrots, some of them forty and fifty years old who had come with the ships. One of them sang "Nearer My God to Thee."

Scene from Maine:

One day this summer our friend took Aggie (Mrs. Rollins) to see Mandy, who's all crippled up with rheumatism. They hadn't seen each other for 37 years. Aggie looked at them sitting down and said, "Two happy women. Two happy women." Aggie said to her, "It wasn't always easy"; and Mandy just screeched at her—"Maybe, but you've got a man to talk to!" Aggie then said, "How's it come about, Mandy, you ain't ever married?" And Mandy said again, and strong, "I wasn't let to; I wasn't let to! Men used to come here, but my father wouldn't have a one of them; it was always 'Wouldn't like to see that man round again, can't see that man again!' And I could have had a house. I know just where it would have been!"

[To his wife, October 1939]

Read the lugubrious and all-guesswork news, and had one good chuckle out of the "Little King"; do save it for the scrapbook; it's grand. After luncheon, I think I may go out to the Brooklyn Museum.

Went to the fair late afternoon and last night, in an

142

atmosphere of New York heat and fog, everybody hot and uncomfortable and the place as crowded thick as a department store basement at Christmas. The Famous Paintings were pretty good, but gave you more a pleasure of recognition than anything else. The best of it was a room of Franz Hals and some fine Italian things—what painters they were, those people! I only stayed about twenty minutes, as the pictures are shown by artificial light in windowless boxes about half the size of Margaret's big room and less high. There was a familiar Vermeer, and some fine David portraits. The rest of the French 18th century and the English 18th century—all ribbons, powdered hair, yellow-haired little Gainsborough infant dukes, etc.— were just millinery, charming millinery.

[To Dr. Neff, April 1943]

Easter is an astronomical feast, an outward expression of man's release from winter and the coming of spring. Would to Heaven that this whole bedeviled, spell-bewitched, war-mesmerized suburb would suddenly reassert its poor humanity, leave the powder and shrapnel factories, and go shouting out those terrible gates, lifting their hands to the sun, and singing hymns to the mystery of rebirth! What men need is not so much a new legal and international scheme for imposing a human rationality on a divine and quite irrational universe, but music, wonder, trumpets and splendors, and the Northern Lights.

[To Dr. Neff, after Allied bombers attacked
Berlin continuously from 21 to 29 November 1943]

I think we have seen, these last few days, the single most appallingly wicked act in all our savage human history. The

143

swift daemonic massacre of some thirty thousand civilians, men, women, and children, the virtual obliteration in vengeance of the greatest single center of our scholarship and western learning, the hideous righteousness, and gloating which has here welcomed the act—was there ever anything more of some Manichee absolute of Evil confronting in equality an absolute of Good? I find, of course, that my belief that the bombing of cities is evil no matter who does it, that cruelty is cruelty always, again no matter who does it, or what its foul and specious "justification" may be—this I find so out of fashion that it is even dangerous to hold. Well—I shall hold it. There may be no such force or phantom as "God" but there is certainly Nemesis as the Greek conceived it in History, and even perhaps the forgotten and quite absurd Furies with their brands of angry fire and their serpent whips. We shall see. But what a world to live in!

Do drop me a line. I have need of it.

[To David McCord]

The skipper of the Maine Seacoast Mission boat has invited me to take a look at the Mission work and go on a cruise with him among the outer islands. I leave on Thursday the 10th, and I understand that I am to go to an island wedding. I once went to the island funeral of a beloved island friend, and I thought it one of the most poignantly memorable of ceremonies. The island was far out in Penobscot Bay, and never shall I forget hearing the bell buoy ringing as we stood gathered in silence at the grave.

*   *   *

"Home is the sailor, home from the sea," and what an adventure it has been! What I shall longest remember is being stormbound Sunday night in the tiny rocky harbor of the farthest out of all the islands, finding myself there in the Maine of 1860 or 1870 without either roads or electric lamps. We were moored against a fish wharf, and as the darkness closed in, it was something elemental, a thing of pitch-blackness full of the roaring of the rising sea and the hollow cry of the gale. No lights on the wharf, no lights ashore save one oil lamp in a fisherman's house and that presently extinguished, nothing but such a hollow of space as must have existed before the creative word brought light into its being. But I must add the contrast. Through this hollow swept at measured intervals followed each by a pause, a great, awesome flare of light from the lonely tower on Matinicus Rock six miles away, the life of the light itself being unseen. As the radiance swept us, I could see the troubled disquiet of the waters in the shelter within, and the almost incredible fury of the sea beyond the breakwater.

How good it is for the human spirit to have a strong awareness, a poetic glimpse of pure chaos and old night! The Rock, surely the most solitary light on the North Atlantic coast, had its tragedy only three weeks ago: One of the keepers, the youngster of the three men, having had his dory picked up and overturned by a giant wave as he was trying to reach the little runway which would have meant safety. He was returning from his liberty. Poor kid!

We put out into the storm the next morning, and grateful was I to the power that endowed me with the best of sea legs! Never have I made so rough a trip. It was like being in midocean in a rowboat, but we had to take the chance or dawdle through another tide. There was a deal of quiet masculine discussion, and out we went. Luckily for us, the wind and the rhythm of the immense waves were "on our tail" as we steered for the land 15 miles away and lost in the speeding vapors of the storm.

145

[To David McCord]

That preposterous old fakir, Elbert Hubbard— how far, far
away all that limp leather and second-rate William Morris
seems! And yet E. H. certainly invented modern American
advertising. C'est son chef d'oeuvre. All those newspaper full-
pages which begin with a picture of Aristotle designing the
Parthenon and end with a blurb about somebody's suspenders—
that's Hubbard.

    We've never recovered from it or him.

[To David McCord, May 1953]

Congratulations on the election to Arts and Sciences! They are
lucky to have you, for a child of arts you are most spiritually,
whilst a paper on something or other of blood—"it will have
blood; they say, it will have blood"—will admit you by the other
great door on a ticket of a different color.

    Give my best to your colleague Miss [Rachel] Carson
who says that The Outermost House is the only book which
influenced her.

    I have been reading Henry James's ghost stories. How good
they are and how unreal, posturings in a noble wallpaper! And
oh! all that twiddling of words like some anonymous insect
twiddling its antennae.

146

[*To his sister-in-law*]

*I have gone back to my first love (or rather first flirtation),
astronomy, and the house is full of astronomical literature and
astronomical almanacs. There is too much moonlight around
this week to get the very interesting world you can pick up
with a field glass, but one can manage a few objects here and
there.*

*Astronomy, war, history, farming and plain cooking—our
days have been passing busily.*

[*To David McCord*]

"Comfort" and "violence" are indeed the pillars of our time.
One presses a button, and a chromium arm reaches out from the
wall to blow one's nose with a "kleanex," and then a moment
later one is shot and robbed in the apartment-house corridor.
Surely, any notion of the perfectibility of "Man" is one of the
most evil of delusions, and I rejoice that the staunchly
conservative Christian churches hold to the admirable doctrine of
original sin.

The other evening my local nephew, Dr. Maclure Day, our
young veterinarian, was called to a lumber camp to attend an
ailing "hoss." He found the creature in the barn, attended to it,
and then going towards his car in the late twilight, saw a second,
seemingly equine, critter, munching hay at the back of the barn.
Something alerted his professional eye, and he took a second
look. It was a gigantic bull moose peacefully sharing hay wisps
fallen on the snow.

[*To Dr. Neff*]

The principal thing I stand for is, I suppose, not a "return to nature," which is a phrase capable of a quite childish interpretation, but the return to a poetic relation to nature. Man is out of relation to his background, and his life has grown spiritually and psychically thin. His blood has grown thin. When man is in poetic relation to his background, he achieves a religious sense of life, and this is the sense that makes him Man. Without a poetic relation to nature and to the sense of his own destiny, he is no better than a woodchuck—isn't as good! Life has no significance in these years, it's only a battle of fierce and confused instincts—all the delightful quality of a street-corner dog fight. And I believe what I italicized in the last chapter of The O. H: "Creation is here and now. We are not living on a mechanism running down like a clock but on an earth sustained by an ever-creating, outpouring stream of the divine imagination." I stand pretty much alone in teaching just this "wisdom," and that's why I have the "public" I seem to hang on to. But do stop me. That delightful parlous pastime of writing about one's self is getting me.

AMERICAN MEMORY

[To David McCord]

I shall long treasure so kind and heart-sustaining a letter. I use the second adjective a-purpose, for in American Memory I thought I had done something really new in spirit and historical approach (in literary design, too) and, moreover, had written (or edited) a book put together with sound scholarship. It is certainly the first essay to take account of America as a place, American history being usually written in vacuo, as if it had occurred somewhere between Polaris and the Great Bear. Whereas it is a product of this tense, oh! so non-European, Red Indian scene with its eternal paradox, in New England, of Roman latitudes and Norway forests and snow. Farther to the south, in the Far South, let's say, one is in the latitude of Africa, in a sunlight that slants down on Dahomey and black kings. I shall continue to hope that one understands America better after reading my book.

[From the Foreword]

Two main currents of American prose reflect the history and the life of the Republic, the one official and literary, the other the contribution of the people. The first has given us the formal literature of the schools, the memoir of the statesman and author, the oration, and our more familiar history; the other,

149

gathering itself from a thousand sources, unstudied, unpretentious, direct, and personal, has given the private letter, the diary in the attic, the little pamphlet peddled in the streets, and the adventure retold for the smaller world of the country newspaper. These things are the bone and blood of any history, and the American material, because of the great variety of adventure inherent in the national life, is, in its way, the richest and most varied in the world. From the beginning, America has been writing about itself, and writing well. Indeed, it is not in the literary imitation of European models that American literature has its deepest roots but in the vigorous narrative prose of the native-born generation who left us their seventeenth-century accounts of Indian captivity.

From the mingling of these streams, using the immediate experience still sharp with emotion wherever I found it, I have put together this memory of the adventure of the Republic, now as then in the making.

[From "First Settlements, the Planter and the Indian"]

The planting of English North America began as a venture of the Elizabethan mind, an exploit of its commerce in the romantic mood, carried on in an English world of seamen and traders whose inherent sense of beauty (especially that of the beauty of speech) and poetic quality of courage were often enough all one with an appalling ruthlessness. Of the new world about to possess them, these Englishmen knew next to nothing. The far country of their imagination was a poem of the times, invented out of the gossip of sailors, and touched with literary color, and its theme was an adventure in wonder and worldly reward.

The unknown land awaited them with power, hidden more than revealed by the daily fierceness of its sun and the Mediterranean slant of its light, and confronting their island souls with the vast natural rhythms and tensions of a continent. South of Cape Cod, it presented itself to their eyes as a low-lying coast backed by an enigmatic forest wall whose only openings were mouths of rivers and the clearings of Indian fields; to the north, the same forest darkened the islands and the cliffs. It was not trackless, but veined throughout with Indian trails and secret paths of war.

Here upon the open coast, near beds of shellfish and where fishing was good, the Indians had their fields of corn and summer villages. By nature hospitable and courageous, notably intelligent within the limits of their experience, at once primitive and ceremonious, and using torture as a kind of terrible ritual, the red men welcomed the unaccountable strangers. Their vice was warfare, continuous and merciless, tribe against tribe, a political weakness which presently delivered them into the hands of the increasing whites; their most irreplaceable quality, their religious relation to the beauty and mystery of the American earth. In their veins ran the blood which had raised the temples of Yucatan; and in some unmeasured past they had discovered or invented the Indian corn.

[From "The Indian Reconsiders"]

To an Indian, the holding of land was a tribal affair, and no Indian was ever quite certain what he was doing when selling it, but the colonist was entirely certain as to what he expected to receive. Confused by English law and punished by it with seventeenth-century rigor, bullied and dispossessed, weakened by new plagues, and his game driven off, the Indian had but two choices if he were not to starve—either to fight or retreat. Further and further back from the sea, increasing along the rivers and Indian paths broken into roads, the cleared land advanced

into the forest. Houses arose in lonely places, Indian corn and
English wheat grew side by side, and the first stowaway weeds
and wildflowers of Europe took their own possession of the land.

[From "War"]

The surprise attack, a favorite device of tribal warfare, was not
long in coming into use, the Indian opposing fire, night, and
terror to the advantage of powder and ball. As early as 1622, a
sudden and general killing of colonists, the "Great Massacre,"
had almost succeeded in restoring Virginia to its original masters;
in New England, King Philip's War—1675 and 1676—was another such attempt at a deliverance, better planned by the tribes,
but made too late. Broken by reprisals, the surviving natives
dwindled away from the occupied portions of the coast, leaving
the whites in possession. Isolated killings, outrages, disputes
ending in murder remained a part of the situation, but the
colonists had time to draw breath. Suddenly the terror began
again. Taking sides with the French established in Canada,
tribes with grievances of their own to redress, descended on the
outlying settlements of the northeast, killing many and carrying
away the rest northward into long captivities.

[From "Geneva and New England"]

The Puritans of New England had come to its shores in no
negative mood of escape; their aim was the founding in the
wilderness of a new, holy, and glorious commonwealth justified
by religion. The measure of all their acts they found in Calvinism, never guessing that it was less a religion than a legal system
whose intellectual interest was the building up of the case of
God against Man. The creation of a powerful mind whose

original interest had been the law, its churches had the cold formality of courts, its ministers the functions of ordained jurists. The logic of this impressive scheme of arbitrary damnation led them back to a deity of blind and incomprehensible will whom they sought in the Old Testament rather than in the New, finding there as well, and taking to themselves, the Hebrew concept of an appointed people wresting a new land from its inhabitants. The liberation of the new and American community from this ancestral ideal of the theocratic state was largely the result of the collapse of the witchcraft delusion, and the following gales of self-reproach and common sense which swept from Massachusetts out over the growing and busy settlements.

The Puritans were English extremists; they stand outside the norm of the English mind, and their true kinship of temper is not with the English but with the Scots. They were moved primarily by ideas, and in the inheritance of this trait lies the living importance of the strain.

[From ". . . Europe on the Trading Paths of America"]

Holding the two great natural gates of the continent, the mouths of the St Lawrence and the Mississippi, the colonial adventure of France had a geographic and strategic magnificence of plan which made the English effort seem haphazard and disorganized. The adventure had begun casually, with the usual explorations and disasters, but presently the genius of Richelieu seized upon it, giving it form and discipline, and making it essentially one of the ventures of the state. Picturesque as it was, at once bold and patient, having both intelligence and "panache," it was true to the French mind in being an idea as much as an outer reality: the coureur de bois and the functionary met upon this ground, and to the achievement of the design came the powerful aid of the intelligence, energy and discipline of the Catholic church.

This was the formidable rival which lay to the north and west of the English colonies, seeking to confine them to the coast. Had the French not incurred the long resentment of the Five Nations, had emigration from France been more plentiful, had the Mother Country been less continuously engaged in wars at home, the historic result would very likely have been a balance of power. But the European wars ignited their new fires in the American woods, the Five Nations spread terror among the French, the French Indian allies sacked the New England and later the western settlements, regular troops entered the picture, and presently a Canada abandoned by a hard-pressed France, fell to the British Crown. The Louisiana possessions were saved from the Lion by a cession to Spain.

[From "The American Scene Takes the Imagination . . ."]

The American does not appear in a generation; the forces of the country needed time to shape him to their will. He is not a figure of the seventeenth century. It is in the eighteenth century that he begins to emerge, a new human being, no longer interested in the resemblances of things American to things European, but in their differences. He has become conscious of America as a place, and aware of the American scale. The huge, sunlit, Red Indian land is his, with its tensions of heat and cold, its tropical violences of summer storm, its incomparable and elegiac autumn, its cloudless winter nights of stars over the wilderness and the snow.

The forest miracle of Niagara, for so many generations the dramatic core of the American scene, the great river, the Mississippi, the Indian mounds of the prairies, the Indian himself, the native and different plant, animal and bird—all these become a part of the conscious heritage: they find their way into books: they bring new pride. The peculiarly American things, the buffalo, the wild turkey, the towering corn, the rattlesnake which so imposed itself upon the architectural imagination of the Central American peoples, the sunflower, the goldenrod—a new awareness of them is at hand; they are part of nationality.

[From "The Age of the Great Rivers"]

The last of the eighteenth century as a living influence fades out of the picture, leaving behind a touch of itself in the power of Jefferson's ideas. A generation born after the Revolution is coming into power—Webster, for instance, and Calhoun, both born in 1782—perhaps the first generation of "Americans" in the modern sense in being the first to be molded by American institutions. A natural turn towards mechanical invention, and an interest in manufacturing owing something to the contemporary scene in England, stir in the national spirit; English locomotives reach the first railroads, and the engines of steamboats are influenced by British design. Cities rise on the lakes in twenty years, not collections of huts, but unaccountable places with broad streets, a planting of trees, buildings of painted brick, and plenty of Greek Revival architecture. The country over, perhaps nothing so holds the people together as their pride in the Union. It has become their poem.

With irresistible strength the nation grows, taking possession of the nearer west with hearth and plough, and driving away the outnumbered Indians in small, inevitable "wars." The Indian Lands bill, 1837, dispossesses the "Five Civilized Tribes" of the South, the Choctaws, Cherokees, Seminoles, Creeks, and Chickasaws, some sixty thousand people, and herds them west to Indian Territory—a greedy and cruel business. There is a side of disorder to the national life which is part of the picture; one reads all too often of mobs and ruffianism and tarring and feathering. But the great force which will ultimately give the new settlements their characteristic faith, which will touch the whole life of the Union with its mores, is already at hand, Methodism, carried ahead with the frontier by the preaching itinerant.

It is the time of the great rivers, the great rivers of the Union, muddy and wide and strong, and flowing through a wilderness which is wilderness no more.

[From "The Golden Age of New England"]

Within twenty miles of Boston and the whaleback islands of the harbor, in its eighteenth-century fields and stone walls, in its New England austerity and quiet, the town of Concord made its adventures spiritual. The Calvinism of New England had faded out of many minds, transforming itself into a Unitarianism whose beginnings were quick with intellectual passion, but the old orthodoxy had not yet given up the ghost, and battling to hold its churches, confronted the new movement, increasingly uncertain as to matters in the heavenly sphere, but very sure about the duty of man on earth. This New England world was touched with the fervor which had touched Carlyle, for New England (unlike the South) had resumed a cultural relation with England, now in her Victorian phase. Parallel to the western movement seeking physical room, there were in New England movements seeking room for the mind, attempts at rural Utopias not too far from Boston, and gatherings of sages intent on building a Yankee Jerusalem in New England's green and pleasant land. Philosophers and poets, men of letters and teachers, these people of the New England Renaissance have the honesty and tang of the apples growing in their orchards, and are equally fruits of their own earth. They ordinarily hitched their Concord wagon to a Concord horse, but were not surprised to find upon occasion that they had hitched it to a star.

[From "Wagon Trails and Pioneers"]

The covered wagon was at once something very old and something American and new. Roofed carts and wagons had accompanied the legions on their marches; they had followed the river
roads of the thirteenth century to medieval fairs; they were a
commonplace of Georgian England, but all had been cumber-
some and heavy in design. It is from this tradition, however, that
there came to be developed in eighteenth-century Pennsylvania,
perhaps from some German hint, the Conestoga wagon with its
boat-shaped body at once handsome and practical; the whole
affair, indeed, being as American in its design as the whaleboat
of New England. Originally intended for the transport of mer-
chandise, it early became a part of emigration, in the beginning
of the nineteenth century carrying New Englanders across the
Berkshires into York State and Ohio, and moving in slow files
along the great national road west out of Baltimore. On the
overland trails, this was the wagon, now turned "prairie
schooner," which came into its own as a part and the symbol of
an epic.

Trappers and explorers had worked out the Oregon Trail, one
man's knowledge supplementing another's; armed parties had
followed it through the mountains. Then came the missionaries
making for the Columbia. The true caravans were a feature of
the Forties, the emigrant parties assembling at St. Louis with
their wagons and steers, their armed horsemen and guides, the
seed corn, the child, and the plough.

[From "The Arrival of the Apprehensive Fifties"]

It was the generation of the daguerreotypes, of those solid men
and women whose glance still confronts us with its air of resolu-
tion. The world they inhabited was not an uncomfortable one,

its furniture was rich and respectably florid, its hospitality substantial, and its manners genteel, but it was haunted day and night by an institution and a question—Southern slavery. Slavery in America was a colonial inheritance descended down into the nineteenth century; outmoded in the rest of the world and repugnant to the moral feeling of the age, in the South it was a familiar part of daily life from earliest childhood, accepted naturally and almost without question. Attempts to interfere with their "peculiar institution"—to use Calhoun's famous phrase—brought to their mind two episodes in history neither far away in time nor place: the ruin of Jamaica by the parliamentary liberation of the blacks, and the horrors of the slave insurrection which had followed the French Revolution in Santo Domingo. To Northern outcries they turned a deaf ear, growing angrier with each pamphlet and speech, and retaliating in their laws by a kind of censorship of Northern ideas. Bitter wrangles over fugitive slaves and congressional struggles between North and South for the cultural possession of the new territories gave the nation no rest. The attempt of John Brown to carry a slave-freeing raid into Virginia darkened the whole Southern mood; if these were abolitionist methods, what next was in store?

[From "The Wild West of the Seventies"]

With his war bonnet of eagle's feathers, his gravity, savagery, and stoicism, it is the Indian of the Far West who has become the Indian of the American imagination. Even the eastern Indian, touched by the national mood, now dons the western war bonnet for festive occasions, although his own ancestors, dwellers in a forest, were usually content with a feather or two arranged in a scalp-lock. The place of the Indian in the American imagination is a part of the history of the American mind. The seventeenth century saw him first as ceremonious and picturesque, a ruler in his own forest, then later as a bloodthirsty demon of the woods; the eighteenth century tended to despise him as a drunken and often dangerous hanger-on, an image gradually transfigured into the Noble Red Man of the lovers of nature, and fixed forever by the genius of Cooper. In the nineteeth century, Catlin and Schoolcraft, journeying westward, had rediscovered him as a man, calling a new attention to the interest and beauty of his primitive arts.

The Civil War at an end, the Nation was now to encounter him on his last frontier—the mounted Indian of the plains on his spotted pony, the hunter of buffalo, the raider, the tragic and perplexed human being, the cunning enemy. It was the Army which won the plains, cavalryman matched against Indian brave; time and the railroads did the rest. Presently the open country was ready for the longhorn and the cowboy, for the American touched with the heritage of Spanish Mexico, the cowboy of romance with his guitar and six-shooter, his Mexican boots and silver spurs, his old-fashioned politeness, and his Spanish words and ballads.

[From "Money, Science, and the City"]

There begins to gather momentum in the Eighteen-seventies an impulse of the American spirit which is later to influence and color the entire life of the nation, the centering of its finance and forces of prestige in the city of New York. The Republic had never had a capital in the European sense, now one began to appear, assuming authority over the arts, setting the social example in the grand manner, and though not the political capital, wielding great political power. The other cities, too, were growing, spreading out into their own suburbs as London had spread a hundred years before, for the dubious gifts of science and the Industrial Revolution were being poured out upon them, calling in the young men from the farms, and the European immigrant from the ships. In this world and its fellow across the Atlantic, money was to appear, perhaps for the first time in human history, as something completely self-justified; the rich man was great in his own right. A real exhilaration of the sense of power began to take hold of the world, the machine could do everything but wrong.

Living, on the whole, more comfortably and grandiosely than it ever had before, the country borrowed its schemes of decoration from contemporary England and its mansard roofs from France, inventing its proportions for itself. Electricity, the foundational force of the technology of the century to come, entered into the service of human life. The American woman, always a little restive at the crude standards of the frontier, and now having money and leisure, attempted the dangerous experiment of setting in moral order a world of men. The South was silent. A promoter began the destruction of the old American splendor of Niagara. The railroads lorded it in the land, the great agricultural machines began to make possible the stupendous farming in the West, and all America went to the first Chicago Fair.

[From "The Times of Theodore Roosevelt"]

Few personalities in modern history have so touched the imagination of a people as Theodore Roosevelt touched that of the Americans of his time. A quarter of a century and a world in murderous confusion have intervened between his age and this, but neither distance nor distraction has managed to wrest his own era from him; sturdy, tireless, full of intellectual curiosity, now addressing his age with the emphasis of a prophet, now delighting it with a boyish gusto of living, and ruling the nation in a style it thoroughly approved of, the figure of Roosevelt stands possessive against the marble and the Roman arches of the great public buildings of his day. It was the golden age of the machine. Nothing needed to be done but to curb the great organizations which were almost empires in themselves, and keep the public conscience roused and battling. The forces of the world had grown gigantic, and where Europe and America met, the City of New York had begun to raise its skyscrapers like a pressure-ridge in polar ice.

The mind of the nation had now become definitely urban, treating the farming countryside more and more as a kind of poor relation whom it was polite to flatter, on Fourth of July occasions, with rhetorical references to Agriculture. The age imagined itself humming like a dynamo, the word coming into use as a complimentary metaphor; the automobile appeared, offering itself both to commerce and the American restlessness, and there began the invasion of the sky. Into the city now poured the new nations and peoples, streaming out in their turn over the old, dark, Red Indian land.

NORTH OF MAINE

A Last Word on *The St. Lawrence*

In between more important work Henry published three little books for children: *Five Bears and Miranda, The Tree that Ran Away,* and *Chimney Farm Bedtime Stories.* Henry could tell the children a story at the drop of a hat. This was part of his Irish inheritance which I admired, for I could never do it. But I could write down a story very easily, sometimes adding a detail here and there. This would have taken Henry far more time than he considered the stories were worth. These small books appeared with as little effort as apple blossoms in May. He didn't consider them to be either his or mine. When they were published he might enjoy looking at them for ten minutes, but I doubt if he ever opened them again.

Far more important was *The St. Lawrence,* about which I have already written. Henry saw the river alone, with me, and for one month with the children, too. He came to know many French Canadians interested in the history and nature of the river. He read about it, thought about it, but above all felt it in all its beauty and power.

Of the many chapters he wrote, my own favorite is that one which celebrates the skies above the river.

THE ST. LAWRENCE

[From "Arrival in New France"]

I came to the St. Lawrence from the wilderness frontier of Maine, crossing again the mountains to which one looks from the top of Jackman Hill; the day was pleasant and it was late in our northern spring. Beyond the town and a last American glimpse, the road climbed a pass into the forest, winding its way north through walls of trees and old clearings full of the quiet of the woods. Presently after some miles of climbing came the more ragged country of the height of land and, by a scatter of tourist shops and signs, the trivial concrete marker of the line.

Here it is that the road descends, passing one of the great divisions of the continent, and Maine and the Republic fall behind together with those streams flowing eastward to the sea. Crossing from an Atlantic slope turned upon the south to one turned upon the north, the traveler has come to a new country, and the light before him is already that of a changed, a colder, and a vaster sky. As he stands facing the mighty northern flowing of the landscape and the great and paler distances of space, the sun is always in the world behind shining with another gleam

166

beyond the height of the frontier. The forest, too, has changed its character. On every side the white pine has given way to the dark masses and tenacities of the more northern spruce, whilst the mountain birch, lover of the north, now towers in new columns above undergrowths of mountain ash and fir. A kind of lumbering which is little more than a sort of ragged gleaning is forever going on here in the forest, and the first houses to be seen are the cabins of the woodsmen by the road.

On the morning of which I write, to one side of a first unpainted shack or house of boards two men were skinning a bear. The poor creature lay extended on an improvised trestle in the sun, a mass of solid, bear-shaped meat emerging from the fur, the skin of a forepaw hanging to one side. The hunters were two young French Canadian frontiersmen in their woodsmen's boots and heavy woolen clothes, and as they worked expertly with their knives, each to his side, a little girl came out of the house to watch, standing and staring in the dooryard with a small child's abstracted reverie.

A little beyond this part of the frontier the road descends a hill cleared of higher timber to the west, and there waits a view which makes as dramatic a transition, I think, as any in the world. To the south whence one has come and to the east at one's right hand rises the barrier of the frontier and beyond it the unseen elms of Maine and all the large ease of the American mood; to the west, like a sort of apparition, stands—France. Some four or five miles away across the gorge of the mountain stream which is soon to become one with the Chaudière is such a village on a cleared hill as one may see almost anywhere in France itself. Distant and grey, massed in something of a silhouette about its church and lifted against an American and northern sky, the nameless hamlet is symbol as well as place, a first outpost, so to speak, of the ancient and traditional agriculture of Europe with its religious mysteries of life and death and the plough. It is poor, it is frontier, but it is the way of life

167

of another world. Beneath their faintest touch of reviving green these fields remain obstinately American; only a thousand upon a thousand years of rain and the patient hand of man will smooth these glacial slopes to the noble contours of the Lyonnais or the Ile de France. But the task has begun, and day by day the land changes while the contemporary years and their violences and shapes pass like the shadows of clouds upon it and are gone.

Here and there, in farm country beyond, great springtide piles of brush were burning, the smoke rolling towards the seasonal rush of the Chaudière, and at a first great field there was going on a venturesome and muddy ploughing. A high wind of spring roared across the land, shaking the boughs of trees just coming into leaf, and blowing away the last of the long cold winter of the north. When the fields had grown warm, in would go the white-flowering buckwheat and the oats, the household patch of tobacco, the kitchen garden with its pride of lettuces, and the possible small field of Indian corn.

There is nothing like following a river to put one into the traveler's frame of mind, and the Chaudière is a good companion. Holding to the road for miles it changes, as one descends, from a mountain rapid to a wide and civil stream. The landscape is now a great cleared valley with hills to each side separated by the river and a floor of meadow lowland; the wilderness (more wood-lot than wilderness) standing with the leftoverness of old snow here and there on farthest heights. Now come towns, the first of the small, picturesque brick and wooden towns of Lower Canada with their small French houses standing sociably side by side along one greater street, maples or poplars in a row, and English sparrows talkative in the leaves. It was pleasant to stop awhile at the entrance to such a place and enjoy the new country, the road, the river, and the sun. On the open slopes across the flowing of the stream were farms and barns, and a road below and a road above, as in the song, whilst behind, coming and going past the poplar trunks, went the butcher, the baker, and the candlestick-maker, each with his lettered cart and good, well-fed comfortable horse. It was by these very roads, I thought, that Arnold's men marched to Quebec, having emerged from the frontier like so many hairy and tattered Ishmaels of the woods. Here, by the stream, under this different light, were the settlements whose people were so kind: it was at these doors that they came knocking in the cold of sunrise or in the first dark of a November night to have hot bowls of soup thrust into their hands and great morsels of the good, life-giving habitant bread. The people in their farms and villages were friendly to the Americans and their venture, wishing them success, but their leaders would have none of it, and kept their little nation faithful to the still new and alien crown.

[*To Dr. Neff*]

We are at a farmhouse near Murray Bay. I have taken half a house, and Betsy and I write in the old French Canadian kitchen, with its huge three-decker French stove, farm chickens stalking the sunlit grass outside, and the mighty landscape of the "Grand Fleuve" visible through the towering spruces to the south. Beautiful country. Last fall I told John Farrar I'd do the St. Lawrence for him in his "Rivers of America" series, and, me voici, Elizabeth and the children are here in charge of a French Canadian nurse, a nice child. Betsy is at the moment doing the proofs of the book edition of "Here I Stay," and I am at the other end of the table, my heart and head full of the thoughts of you and yours.

I shall presently be deep in chapters, and after the long strain of last winter, I think I'd better stay lost in this new interpretation, indeed, I'll have to! I've eaten so much country maple sugar recently, and spoken so much French, that I shall presently be indistinguishable from a French Canadian.

169

[From "The American Captives"]

The War of the Spanish Succession, which began in the great apartments at Versailles, was not long in reaching the granite ledges of the New England coast. With hostile Indians and the paths of the forest at their backs, and French Canada at the end of those paths, the frontier settlements of the coast of Maine stood in particular peril of destruction.

On August 10, 1703, at nine o'clock of a pleasant summer's morning, a band of French and Indians made a surprise attack on the village of Wells. Painted like devils from some aboriginal Hell and sounding that strange Indian ululation of war, that clear, birdlike piping which has the terror of the nonhuman, the Abenakis went swiftly to their looting and killing. Soon many of the houses were in flames. When the attack slackened, some thirty-nine of the inhabitants had either been killed or captured. The Indians then gathered their prisoners together, the men, women and little children standing to one side in their forlornness and anxiety, and turning them from the smoke and the August sea, marched them off into the unknown country of the woods.

The village, making a list of the missing, presently discovered that a little girl of seven had been carried away by the raiders. This was Esther Wheelwright, daughter of John and Mary Wheelwright, and granddaughter of the Puritan minister who, with his friends, had founded the town. One sees her as a child of the frontier yeomanry moving against the background of some great colonial hearth with its blackened pots and wooden spoons, its birchbark containers and its English knives. Two years pass, and a letter from an American prisoner in Quebec brings news that some of the captives from Wells are in the city. Esther was not mentioned. Where, then, was she? Had so small a person died somewhere on the long march through the wilderness?

170

More years passed, and there was still no news from Canada. Esther was not in New France. For some reason or other her Indian captor (whose personal property she happened to be) had not sold her to the French, but kept her in an Indian village in the wilderness of the upper Kennebec. For six years she had lived as an Indian, wearing the rags and tatters of their clothes and speaking their tongue. It was in this situation that she was discovered by a kindly and pious missionary priest, Father Bigot, and was by him ultimately ransomed from her captors.

Then came a great and surprising change. Arriving on the St. Lawrence, the little "Englishwoman" was given over to the hospitable care of two great personages, de Vaudreuil, the governor of New France, and his lady. From the forest and the primitive noise and dirt of an Abenaki village, Esther Wheelwright passed to the French decency and order of the governor's own house. She was then a girl of twelve or thirteen. On January 18, 1709, Mme. de Vaudreuil brought the child to the Ursulines. "Madame La Marquise brought us a little anglaise as a pupil," says the register. The New England connection, it would seem, had become somewhat nebulous, though it was to assert itself later and be touchingly and dutifully respected.

Far away in New England, John and Mary Wheelwright had been having other children. Including Esther, there had been eleven altogether. Under the care of the Ursulines, some deep religious sense woke in the child, and she accepted Catholicism with fervor and fell easily into the French way of life. Yet de Vaudreuil would not allow her to take the first steps of her profession as a nun. Not till October 2, 1712, after two years of complicated negotiations concerning all prisoners, years in which Esther does not seem to figure, did Father Bigot's protégée begin her novitiate at the Ursulines' of Quebec. The old priest insisted on paying all the expenses of the ceremony. "Thy hand shall lead me and thy right hand shall hold me," was his text.

That Esther's family knew where she was is clear. A note in

the original records of the Ursuline community states that following the girl's profession as a nun her family in New England were notified, and that they responded lovingly "with letters and gifts."

She was now la Soeur Esther Marie Joseph de l'Enfant Jésus. In the convent above the St. Lawrence the placid and ordered life of a French religieuse gathered a Puritan into its ancient routine of teaching and prayer. The long years and the long winters passed over the Rock. In January 1754, when Soeur Esther was in her fifty-eighth year, a young man who had come up from Boston through the Maine woods most unexpectedly presented himself at the convent door. It was a colonial officer, Major Nathaniel Wheelwright, her brother's son, and he had arrived in Quebec to discuss an exchange of prisoners taken in the frontier skirmishes which had been fought in America during the years of nominal European peace. The young man gave his kinswoman—"my Aunt Esther Wheelwright"—a miniature of her mother painted as a young woman, and presented to the Ursuline community "a silver flagon, some fine linen, and a silver knife and fork and spoon."

Then came the siege and its bombardments, its fires and destructions, and final battle on the heights and the death of Montcalm. At the beginning of hostilities—the Ursuline convent being very exposed to cannon fire—the community of nuns had taken refuge at the Hôpital Général. Eight sisters, however, remained at the convent itself to take what care they could of their endangered home. Their quarters were in the great cellars of the buildings and they could hear through the rock the detonation of the shells. Soeur Esther Marie, then a woman of sixty-seven, was one of this group. In the terrible silence which lay upon the city after the defeat upon the plains, the body of Montcalm was brought at night from the house of the surgeon Arnoux to the chapel of the Ursulines. There, by candlelight, amid the sound of Latin and while all wept, they buried him in an opening of the foundations an enemy shell had pierced beneath the wall. Holding their tapers, the sisters stood to one side, their dark habits massed in somber contrast to the bright colors of the military attendants, while unseen and unheard the great river seemingly carried away in the night the last fragment of the national and religious dream.

In December 1760, three months after the capitulation at Montreal, Soeur Esther Marie was elected superior of the Ursulines of Quebec. The anxiety, poverty and distress which shadowed all French Canada had not spared the community. Moreover, its buildings were in ruin. Wherever a chimney was still usable and a roof intact the sisters gathered together. Finding that the British officers had a fancy for the French and Indian handicraft of embroidery on birchbark, they kept busily at their needles, embroidering card cases and birch what-nots for the young, half-frozen subalterns. The community was desperately poor, and the life of the entire colony tragically disorganized. As a leader of the French, it was more than once the new superior's duty to discuss matters of policy with Sir John Murray, their new British governor.

The spirit of history, were it present, must have thought it a strange and ironic meeting. On the one side stood the venerated abbess, an "anglaise" by blood, granddaughter of that bold and combative Puritan, the Reverend John Wheelwright of the Lincolnshire fens and the wild New England coast; on the other stood Murray in his general's uniform, a Scottish younger son from a castle near Dranmore. There is something very likable about Murray. His letters reveal a nature essentially understanding and kind; as far as he could be he was a friend as well as a conqueror, and he dared much to protect the French from the commercial "harpies and bullies"—the phrase is his—who came settling out of the air to exploit the new prey. The world into whose colonial echoes Esther Wheelwright had been born, the British community with its redcoat values and staunch

173

Protestantism, that society which lives for us in Hogarth and the incomparable "conversation pieces" of Zoffany, had conquered the world into which a caprice of history had led the little child from Wells, and to the service of whose purposes she had dedicated her entire life. Now it was all over, or seemed all over, with the only world she had ever really known. The pomp of Versailles, the great altars and the fluted columns, the august sound of eighteenth-century religious song, the white flag with the lilies, and the soldiers with gauntleted and embroidered gloves—all this must have seemed withdrawing like music into a sadness of distance far from her undaunted New England head. Flags, she may have thought, were but a part of time: she would serve the timeless to the end.

She died in 1780 at the age of eighty-four. There is much about her in the annals of the Ursulines, and a number of her letters are in existence. They reveal her as a fine and thoughtful person meeting with wisdom and good-tempered fortitude the disasters of her world. Still in use, but not shown, is the silver flagon her nephew put into her hands in the convent parlor on a Quebec winter morning close upon two hundred years ago. The little miniature of her mother may be seen. It has been retouched, a kind of saint's veil has been arranged about the head, and there is a story, perhaps a legend, that this was done in order that Esther Marie might keep this family picture with its ties and memories of "the world."

The most interesting relic, however, is in New England. It is the portrait of Esther Wheelwright as abbess of the Ursulines. Painted in 1761, it was sent by the abbess to her mother, who had lived on to advanced age. Painted in Canada when La Tour was painting in France and Reynolds in England, no portrait could be less of the eighteenth century: in manner and spirit there is not a touch of the contemporary European world. It is a pure seventeenth-century canvas, even such a likeness as the first Massachusetts Puritans bequeathed to their descendants to measure them and their times with their obstinate and formidable glance. The dignified, wise and self-reliant visage of the woman of middle age who looks at us out of her Ursuline coif does its own honor to so resolved a heritage. The power is there and the character, but there is no harshness in the firm mouth, no defiance of life and kings in the large eyes and assured and disciplined gaze. In the darkened canvas France and New England meet and are at peace.

[From "The Golden Age of the Canoe"]

No adventure of the Canadian past so stirred the heart as the departure of the voyageurs from their depot at Lachine. One came upon them in the busy spring, some camping by the river in the open fields, Montreal and its church bells behind them to the east, and before them the afternoon sun and the adventure of the west. For days before the embarkation wagons had been arriving with their loads, rolling through the farming villages and deepening the ruts and puddles with their weight of trade goods, provisions and supplies. In and out of the offices and wharves, busy at a hundred tasks, yet always finding a moment to toss back a jest, swarmed the adventurers, a whole French Canadian countryside of Gaspards, Aurèles, Onesimes, and Hippolytes. There was much to be done. Here, on the beach, men crouched by a canoe making some last repair, here clerks scrambled over boxes and bags checking and rechecking the trading goods, the trinkets, beads, axes, knives, awls, blankets, and bolts of bright red English flannel, here an official studied the enlistment papers of some new engagé. At a counter to one side, a crowd selected the shirts, trousers, handkerchiefs, and blankets due them from the company, Iroquois Indians from Caughnawaga, famous paddlemen, reaching in and seizing with the rest. Late in the afternoon, those who were quiet over a pipe

175

could hear the eternal murmur of the miles of rapids, and the floating, clanging summons of the Angelus.

The moment of departure waited upon weather and the wind. To prevent a last and too-thirsty festival of farewell, efforts were sometimes made to conceal the probable day, but men concerned have sixth sense in these matters, and the world was apt to share the secret, and all Montreal, finding the morning fair, came to say goodbye. Ladies with escorts watched from the shores, British officers, mounted on English horseflesh, rode to good places in the fields, British soldiers even, their flaxen hair and blue Sussex eyes a new note in the throng, strolled in pairs among the Indians. Citizens and citizenesses, wives and children, parents and kin, company directors and curés—all these were at hand to see the start. It was early May, and the Montreal country had left winter behind and was taking courage in the spring; on far shores and near, under the cool wind, appeared the green.

In and out of the press, heroes of the occasion, moved the voyageurs. Old hands and new, it was their day. Even the young Scots clerks who were to go as passengers to the forts shared the importance and the glory. Custom demanding that the beginning and end of a journey should be carried off in style, every voyageur was dressed in the best he had. A woolen tunic or long shirt worn outside and belted about with a bright, home-woven sash—the charming, old-fashioned ceinture flèchée—Indian leggings or even homespun trousers, a red knitted cap, and heavy-duty Indian moccasins—this was the costume. A beaded Indian pouch worn at the waist, Iroquois or Chippewa work, was a particular *sine qua non*: indeed, all veterans were engayed with Indian finery. Voyageurs belonging to the governor or chief factor's brigade had feathers in their caps. Often a small British flag was flown from each canoe. The fleet sailed by "brigades," by groups under one command, and these kept together, maneuvering with careful paddles in the current falling to the Lachine.

Are all afloat, all loaded, all officers and passengers in their seats? Then go! Church bells rang, guns were fired, and on the broad river paddles dipped and thrust forward in a first strong, beautiful and rhythmic swing. At the same moment the river covered itself with singing. The fleet beginning to open, the brigades sorting out, one could see nothing but canoes for miles, hundreds upon hundreds of the laden craft all striking as one into the purplish-brown waters of the Ottawa.

At the northwestern corner of Montreal Island stood a church of Ste. Anne, patroness of sailors and of voyageurs. Here the brigades made a first halt and landing, the paddlemen and bowsmen, the steersmen, clerks and passengers all trooping up from the beach to pray for a safe voyage and a safe return. It was the custom to make some small offering, and the Scots Presbyterians, it is said, made theirs in propriety with the rest. Soon they were all of them on the river again, the church hidden by some turn of the stream, some brigades falling into their measure and stroke, some out of high spirits leaping ahead with a song, "en roulant, ma boule, roulant," and out of sight they go. Thrust by thrust, by quiet waters and by furious streams, through the summer plague of the stinging flies and the blessed coming of the early cold, the paddles will swing across the half of a continent, making their way into the forest, into the land of Keewaytin, the northwest wind, the ancient land where nothing has changed since the beginning of the world.

[From "Ontario to Montreal"]

It is the York State St. Lawrence, the river with Ontario and Britain on one side, and the United States and Congress and the Presidents to the other. To the Canadian north are old farms and fields with willows bordering their shores and silvering in the wind. Here and there, in crannies of the bank under a decorum of leaves, are old-fashioned cottages playful with architectural gingerbread, and from time to time appear small rustic towns whose houses and trees seem to have been planted together in some Canadian moment of the mid-Victorian mood. The landscape reflects a way of life less hurried than the American. Town halls have even something of a British propriety, and the bells in the brick churches strike noon with a measured and English air.

Across the stream, under the same inland light, the same level distances of grassland and trees fall back from the yellow earth of the New York shore. The farms seem more scattered and uneven and are farther from the river, towns count for less, and there are more groves of elms standing green beside the bank. It is not the landscape of the shores, however, which now seizes upon the imagination of the traveler. For thirty miles he has been following a great and single channel direct as some vast canal, a line of water drawn across a part of North America as it might be across the face of Mars. So evenly between its banks does it keep its average width of a fair two miles that the long, natural perspective has even something of an artificial air; one might be in the presence of some great work of the ancient and mysterious America of the Mound Builders. Looking westward from Prescott in Ontario one sees a surprising sight at the far end of the fairway. It is a sea-like horizon on a river, a level line of water and sky suspended in space between the substantiality of parallel shores, themselves vanishing over the rounding plunge of earth.

Flat wavelets speckle the channel, flicked from the current by the inland breeze. Eastward and ahead, vast steps in the rush of the river downhill from the lakes, lie the great rapids, the roar of their narrow caldrons, long slopes, and wider seas of fury soon to break upon the listening ear.

Only the strong current, eddying in deep mid-channel and

178

flowing like a long and hastening ripple past the banks, carries a hint of what is presently to come. The river has quickened pace into new country, an open table-land of grass and gravel down whose yellow banks glacial boulders have here and there rolled to the water's edge; the great main channel is over and done; ahead, level islands of the stream's own making bar and turn it in its gathering and meandering rush. It is farming land, and there are cattle on the islands, black-and-white Holsteins feeding under the willows and the grovelike beauty of the elms. A touch or two of industrialism on the Canadian side, and the beginning there of the canal world does not change the character of the landscape or the emphasis of its way of life. The river, which at Prescott and Ogdensburg was a pale and inland blue, has in this yellower earth gathered a tinge of green.

Lake freighters coming and going to Montreal have gone into the canals. Slow dignities of hulk and painted iron, they move along the separate water, their stacks visible in the distance above and through the trees.

The islands are now close at hand, lying in the stream like hindrances in a corridor, and confusing the descent with turns and passages about and between their steeper-growing banks. Alongside, the water is now plunging forward in a rush, boiling up from below in circles like huge lily pads expanding. Two rapids which are little more than a new and fiercer hurrying under the keel pass by without drama of sight or sound. More rapids follow and a long rush at whose far end a growing roar overflows into the blue and casual day.

A shudder, a strange motion downhill into a vast confusion and a vaster sound, and one is in the pool which is the climax of the Long Sault. So steep is the winding rush downslope into the pool and out of it along a furious curve, that the rims of water close along the banks stand higher than the tumult in the pit, and one passes, as it were, through banks of water as well

179

as banks of land. Currents and agitations of wind, rapids of the invisible air, enclose the ship in a leap, scurrying the deck with their small and wild unrest. In the caldrons all is giant and eternal din, a confusion and war and leaping-up of white water in every figure and fury of its elemental being, the violence roaring in a ceaseless and universal hue and cry of water in all its sounds and tongues. The forms of water rising and falling here, onrushing, bursting, and dissolving, have little kinship with waves at sea, with those long bodies of the ocean's pulse. They are shapes of violence and the instancy of creation, towering pyramids crested with a splash of white, rising only to topple upstream as the down-current rushes at their base. Lifted for an instant of being into a beauty of pure form and the rising curve, they resemble nothing so much as the decorative and symbolic waves of the artists of Japan.

Enclosing the pool, in a strange contrast of mood, stands an almost sylvan scene, a country shore of grass and trees and a noontide restfulness of shade.

A bold turn of a gravel promontory, and one escapes out of the caldron into a broadening reach of calmer water. Widening, widening to a lake, the river achieves an afternoon peace, and there comes slowly into view a landscape so much part of the old beauty of the past, a landscape so poignantly and profoundly American, that time seems to have stood still awhile above the river.

[*From a St. Lawrence notebook*]

Cataract

The old America—I was reminded of this subject by a visit to the Chute de Seigneur, a ravine cleft in the brownish-grey

180

*volcanic rock; nobody to bother you, no papers or nastiness
about, nothing but Nature.*

*The overfall of water with the sun shining through to the
lacy streams of water falling, or rather running, down over the
channeled rock beneath. This seen only in direct sunlight—*

*Noticed that the falling and hurled water had a sideways turn
as it fell, a little twist clockwise; but my eyes grew disordered
as I watched and when I turned away, the rocks below heaved
like a stage sea.*

[From "St. Lawrence Sky"]

Over this landscape of mountains and climbing roads, over this
great river with its shores of farming lands and gathered villages
stands a sky which, more than any other sky I have chanced to
live beneath, is blended into a noble unity with the earth below.
It is not in its essence a sky of clouds at all or even a sky of
cloud, but a sky of primordial vapor of cloud, an elemental substance and presence of the mist dwelling in the northern air
and in these winds, and seemingly arriving out of nowhere and
into nowhere vanishing. It achieves a kind of form, becoming
one dense and universal body during the night; it returns to
formlessness with the warmth of the morning sun, dissolving to
a texture in the air. Now, and only too often, a melancholy
pall of rain and fog filling the whole sodden world with the deep-
toned solitary cries and answering choruses of the bewildered
and invisible ships, now a wild aerial wrack floating like rolling
smoke across the silver-whitened sun, it can make of any one
day a wayward series and variety of days. Dramatic, unpredicta-
ble, and very great in its own aspects of beauty, the sky is here an
integral part of human life and the day's experience, a mystery
touching every thing that lives with its fantasies of change.

It is the vapor mass of the lower St. Lawrence to which one

looks, that continent of water and air born of the entrance of the colder sea into the channels of the earth, a mystery of currents and tides and of the warming and cooling of these northern surfaces and the outlying ocean streams. Once the fierce openness of winter is at an end, and the cold and laggard spring comes over the snow with mud and rain and the sound of forest cataracts, the mystery gathers, standing dark in the wilderness sky or drifting down upon the river in its first advancing tongues. So protean is its nature, however, that it seldom occasions a true summer of grey skies. What it brings into being, especially during the early summer, is a sky all vapor and light and fantasy overhead and an earth immersed in transparencies of vapor and cloudy light as in a sea. A paler sun shines, the torn and transparent wraiths drift over the vast contours of the earth, arriving from the north and east and from over the empty mountains, hour by hour rolling off like smoke from some monstrous fire of the gods.

Passing over at a height of some seven or eight hundred feet, and keeping well above the landscape in its drift, it is cloud wrack for all nearness, having neither the look nor the character of fog. As it flows, a new experience and pleasure await the eye. So vague, so unsubstantial are the beautiful and fragmentary shapes that cloud shadows do not follow them below, resting upon the solider earth with the antique majesty of the air. It is a new drama, a drama of light, which now appears in the wide scene. Out of some wild tatter of the veil, swimming as with its own motion forth from a vaporous obscuration, the sun of noon and afternoon is forever palely adventuring, taking to itself some sudden aspect of the countryside. Now it is a farmhouse with its woods and fields which stands enclosed in the pool of burning yet dewy light, now an island in the river, now perhaps a field of charlock in flower far up among the hills. Near and far, village and field, all is substantial: there is no sense of blur, but the

182

air and the mood of nature are touched with water and the spirit, with romantic solemnity and the northern dream.

Beautiful as they are, the colors of this sky are cold. There is but little red in it at any season or hour and the touches of rose which came at sundown have a way of appearing in the east. Fog or gathered cloud, the sky remains a tableau of the tones and austerities of grey intermingled with a northern blue and a rather cold and silvered white. There is an evening gold on the mountains to the west, but it vanishes swiftly and without warmth into the dark.

Inland winds from the west and southwest blowing hot and dry are hostile to this sea of wrack, but winds from the ocean favor it, and strengthening it with ocean fog, roll the mingling masses before them up the river. I once saw such an oncoming, the very sky itself all storm and darkness to the east, advancing up the river like a wall. Pressing forward in a towering solemnity of huge and opaque densities, streaming vapors and wild aerial wrack, on it came, advancing between the darkening mountains westward into the open sunshine of the other half of day. Eastward, in and below the mass, the country streamed with rain. In spite of it, work continued in the fields and on the roads, the huddled groups, the solitary figures laboring on in the wet, for the habitant makes but little of rain and faces all but the very sluice gates of Heaven with his patience and endurance. Coming out of the deeper woods, I saw in a first field to the right, a young man ploughing with a black bull and a black horse harnessed side by side; back and forth through mud they ploughed, opening their rainy land under the deepening and the thinning showers. And because it was baking day, the fires in the outside ovens were burning fiercely in their caves, their smoke and flame licking out of the doors into the streaming of the rain.

Coming out of the mountains to the lower road, I left for a

moment the storm behind me, and from somewhere above the Isle of Orleans beheld Quebec in the distance still enclosed in a pleasant summer light of the later afternoon. The overtaking storm again drew near; it began to sprinkle and grow dark, a churchly and familiar sound of bells suddenly gave a voice to the land, and from the next height of the road, above a river silvering and misting to a ghost, there was no more a distance or a city.

[*To his wife*]

I found the "Moteur Vapeur" Matane at her dock at about nine in the morning, and so cold and grey and Decemberish was the day that all of us, sailors and all, thought sure it would snow. The dock was an interesting picture, for the Matane was carrying over to the Côte Nord about 75 or 100 French Canadian lumberjacks or woodchoppers assembled by various "jobbeurs" to cut wood for the great pulp companies. And so there they were in their bottes sauvages, their heavy army-style "britches," their colored socks and checked windbreakers— black-and-white checks, red-and-white checks, tan-and-blue checks, fake leather, too—and all sorts of old clothes. Farmers, and poor farmers' sons, said the ship's officers—"the poor," the hardy and hard-working younger men, scattered through with the voyageur-lumberjack type. There was Indian in a lot of faces, others were Scotch and Irish looking, husky, red-haired, blue- to green-eyed, and all talking French. Every man came aboard with his great pack on his back, of clothes, blankets, and so on, often with an axe-handle sticking out of the flap. The poor, patched devils had all their worldly goods stowed in an invariable fertilizer sack tied to the shoulders with a bit of coarse string. So there was a great stir of departure, with autos rolling up, men arriving, jobbeurs, agents or bosses giving out pink travel tickets, a dog or two looking interestedly on, and

184

amid the crowd on the wharf looking down, various "lady friends," that's about the nuance.

But it was picturesque, and it reminded me of war days, the crowded, large-puppyish men, the sense of potential hardness and power, the vibration of adventure. That chap whom you and I saw once from the car, he who looked so like Edward VIII, was among them; he is sui generis, and would have been recognizable anywhere! And as a background, this absolute December, which, avoiding snow after all, presently turned to fog and occasional rain.

I had little sleep either night, for the first night, all night long, after a wild passage across the fleuve, we kept stopping at little forlornities, on the edge of this vast uninhabited wilderness— a house or two, a disused pulp wharf, a glare of leftover electric lights, a few people standing distractedly by, and, all around, the vast, rain-drenched pitch dark of the wilderness.

The second day, in fog thickening slowly, we retraced our steps, and finally had to spend the next night floating somewhere in mid-fog, in midstream, unable to get within miles of Matane. The vibration of the little steel tub was terrific, the Diesels shook her just like an eggbeater, making everything loose not clatter but ring with a wild incessant buzz, partitions and all— while the ventilator screamed, really screamed like a devil who has been sprinkled with holy water. It was a grim night each way, and I doubt if anybody bothered to undress. The cuisine, by Heaven's decree, was amazingly good!

We arrived at Matane this morning in a wild downpour of rain, twelve hours late, and I came back to the Hotel Belle-Plage to get a bit of rest, and try to work out a possible plan of going on to the Gaspé if the weather clears. The fog has been pea-soup all day, rushed through with furious showers. Nous verrons, and I'll telegraph again.

The officers of the ship were a nice lot and gave me some picturesque information about le fleuve in winter.

[*To Dr. Neff*]

Labrador and Newfoundland were memorable places. The first named presents a dramatic contrast between the barrenness of the summerless, cold, fog-overladen land and the teeming richness of the sea; the second, at first view, might be St. Brendan's Island, all mountain shapes and loneliness, and a cold ocean breaking on sheer walls, but within, it is forlorn, and the pulp towns are the most hideous conglomerations of diseased ugliness that human beings have ever made to live in. To think that the averred images of God had so lost both their divine and human inheritance, gave me a philosophic melancholy.

[From "Indian Pilgrimage"]

In certain of its aspects, a journey beside the great St. Lawrence is an adventure beyond politics and frontiers into the older America of the forest, the cataract, and the shadow of trees, an adventure into the pages of *The Last of the Mohicans*, and within sound of the grave and romantic voices talking in the immemorial quiet of the woods. It is something of a pilgrimage, too, into the America of the late eighteenth- and early nineteenth-century colorists and engravers where the Indian and his wife and a child stand by a forest stream and a red-coated soldier bargains for a trinket sewn with beads. What a blessed quiet reigns in such old scenes, drawn before the age of violence and squalor had emerged from the hands of the Devil, its father! One can almost hear a leaf fall, touching other fallen leaves with a last delicate scratch of sound, or the purling of the brook flowing with such sylvan decorum through the glade.

It is to the artists of Britain that we owe the preservation of such charming and old-fashioned glimpses of the older continent, for the young men from London were touched by the landscape in its virginal and mysterious splendor and crossed the Atlantic to paint it in Canada, returning home with canvases and water-colors which the great engravers and printers of mezzotints made popular in the ceremonious Georgian world. Indeed, to this very day, in the windows of those printshops just to one side of Piccadilly, Niagara still plunges green and white in its eighteenth-century sublimity, whilst the Indian and the Redcoat, enclosed in a portfolio, wait but a request to revisit the London day.

Always the Indian; of that figure every nation and indeed every age has had its dream. The romance of the American Indian is part of the history of the Western mind. It is worthy of note that it was not the Indian of the great barbaric civiliza-tions to the south, not the Aztec noble or the Peruvian in his woven mantle, who captured the world's imagination, but the wild man to the north, the tawny hunter in his moccasins, the painted savage crouching by the fire. The first lines of the composite figure show us the Algonquin of the coast, the pencil sketching-in a picturesque figure coming to greet strangers with a certain ceremoniousness and a natural turn for trading and sociability, a first portrait which the bitter struggles and mas-sacres to come never quite erased from European memory.

The Jesuits of France and Canada are the next to work from life, being the first Europeans to know the northern "Indian" from intimate association with his flea-bitten dogs and smoke-filled lodges. Here the lines are less favorable, the truly heroic pages of the *Relations* depicting an Iroquoian primitive for whom the fathers would have enthusiastically pre-empted Mr. Kipling's famous "half devil and half child." Appalling as was the life portrayed, seeming even now a mixture of the Stone Age and hell, the accounts brought the "Indian" out more clearly, and succeeded in touching with power the imagination and the piety of France. Thus little by little the figure takes shape, character and light and shade adding themselves to the drawing, till presently that honorable dream, the Noble Savage, comes with dignity from the painted forest and the rainbow on Niagara.

That a child of Nature, a creature of the instinctive self and the untutored mind, should be a noble being is surely a dream which does honor to the imaginative soul of man. The idea conceals a certain criticism of civilization, for if the man of the woods could be such a fine fellow, of what use was the world's baggage of institutions and forms? Yet the most interesting thing about the Noble Savage (which has been too little remarked upon) is the fact that, to a notable degree, the figure was real. The Noble Savage was noble and he was a savage. The Stone Age Iroquoian primitive had in a scant hundred years crossed the astronomical abyss between the Neolithic and the age of Louis Quinze. What primitive people have ever done as much in a century of history? The Jesuit fathers would have scarcely known their man. This is the figure which so moved Franklin and Benjamin West; this is the chieftain and warrior with his gorget of silver and his blanket of finest London wool; this is Uncas as both ideal and human being. What is unreal is not the figure but the Nature out of which he comes. It is the Nature of literary convention, the Nature of contemporary literature, an image of the gardens of Versailles and St. James's Park, the intense thread of violences and cruelties having been sentimentally removed from the formal and pompous tapestry. Yet look again at the figure brushing aside the blue-green and woven leaves, a circular crown of feathers on his head; wait but another moment, and the tapestry boughs will presently melt into the great eighteenth-century trees of Pennsylvania, and the figure, changing and drawing near, be seen as flesh and blood.

With the eighteenth-century passing of the Indian as a political force, the eighteenth-century "Indian," feathers and all, dissolves out of life to live on in literature. Of the Noble Savage presently only the dream remained. (Thanks to Cooper, en-

188

tranced adolescents were to read of him in every European tongue.) To exist in reality, the figure had to be free to be an Indian, the Stone Age and the eighteenth century managing some kind of picturesque and happy blend. Encircled after the Revolution by the hunger and advancing pressure of the whites, the Indian of the east shrank back to the last meager relics of his lands, no longer defending them by arms but by contests of law. Through the open windows of courthouses built in the Greek Revival manner, the sonorous oratory of Indian chieftains in blue broadcloth and silver buttons floated out into a world whose quiet the first railroad engines were presently to disturb with a first imperious bell.

So began the new times, the long years of powerlessness, estrangement, and unheralded fortitude. The Algonquin of the coast, the seventeenth-century Indian, was gone. He existed, he had his tiny islets and even a village or two almost all his own, but the pressure of the surrounding world had weakened his hold on his own way of life, and he was only too often a basket-selling ghost in a Daniel Webster hat. In this State of Maine, in the early nineteenth century, small family bands sometimes came to ask leave to camp in some wooded cove of a favorite lake, and would spend the summer there, an open fire twinkling at night on the beach by the canoes. In the autumn, gift was returned for gift, and on some late September night when Capella was rising higher over the cleared rye-fields and the first farms, some friend would look from a kitchen window and see no fire on the shore.

Our Indian arts of the higher Northeast are far more primitive, and represent the crafts of a hunter people living a primitive and nomadic life. Each little gathering made what it needed, and humanized the thing made with some simple decoration. Birch-bark and porcupine needles, basket strips of the white ash, bone, spruce root, sinew, hide and stone—there was so little to work with. The birchbark, however, lent itself interestingly to design,

189

creating a style which was all its own of silhouettelike figures of the larger forest animals. Limited as were its materials and various the nature of its design, what one feels in the art is an essential humanity. It is as near nature and as much a part of nature as the print of a foot beside a pool. And once these simpler peoples had been introduced to European beads and techniques, they evolved an art whose sense of color and floral design is in itself a unique flowering of the human spirit.

The eighteenth century had moved on: the nineteenth was daily taking shape as the white man's very own. The continent was his where he chose to go. So complete was the victory across the more temperate and exploitable latitudes that the invader himself forgot that the continent was greater than the shadow of his hand. Beyond the noise of his industries and the overflow of his power waterfalls, beyond the steely tenor of the circular saw greedily destroying the great archaic forest, beyond the seas which remained open in winter and beyond their skies, the immense American north, almost half the continent, remained as a shelter for the past.

Inaccessible and cold, too short of summer for the plough and too rocky for the furrow, its timber spindling out to the vast wastes of the barrens, the north invited neither conquest nor conqueror. It was a wilderness, a thing with its own primeval devils, a solitude curving up over the earth from the waters of the St. Lawrence to the Pole. It had belonged to the Indian in the prehistoric past, his it would remain. More than any other part of the continent it is still his today. Only in that vast nothingness will you find the red man (and I speak here of the Algonquin of the forest) without that mask those of us who have shared his lodges know he wears when our white world has enclosed him and turned the key, that mask which no word of his betrays of a concealed, patient, and reflective hopelessness. In the north the landscape is still Indian, and Canadian liners on the homeward run, entering the noble Strait of Belle Isle, see to the west the austere and unpeopled coast of the first discoverers.

Behind that rim of surges there are none to hear; beyond that first meager and twisted wall of the forest, live the Montagnais and the Nascapi, kindred people, the northernmost of the Algonquins. Farther west, in the thousand upon a thousand miles to the north of the lakes, dwell the Chippewas and the roving Crees, the short, dark people of the higher wilderness. The whole vast region is under the authority of the white man's law, administered with justice and power, but the earth forces of the wilderness are archaic and hostile, having as little to do with law and the white spirit as a billow of sleet in a gale. It is the Indian's America.

The St. Lawrence had turned into a sea. Eastward lay a seeming ocean and an horizon; to the south, the last blue island of the south shore had vanished below the curve of water and the earth. Spreading out our charts on deck, we estimated that the northern tributary into whose river mouth we were bound lay about two-thirds of the way eastward from Quebec to the opening of the gulf, and it was near. Appearing with inconsequential suddenness, a red church presently came into a view across the water of an opening bay, and a line of small, unpainted houses projected itself between sea and sky on the August afternoon. It was Bersimis, the large village of the Montagnais Indians of the Côte Nord. The water began to discolor with the forest brownness of the fresh, inflowing stream. Rounding a great horn of river sand, and exchanging our sea eyes and consciousness for the restored perspectives of the shore, we drew up to a large wharf on the tributary.

Looking about, I thought to myself that Indian settlements in the north have all of them a family identity. There is sure to be a church, a store or two, a trading post of a fur company, the quarters of the government officials, and the scattered, unpainted shacks of the Indians. Sometimes there are tents beyond the houses: there were none here. At Bersimis, as in other places, the community stood isolated against the wilderness, a rendez-vous of human beings holding their own between the empty horizons of the river and the gaunt and final wall of the north woods.

I had heard of the village from various friends. It was difficult to reach by either land or sea. The last road in the Northeast ended at Portneuf beyond the Saguenay, leaving the real wilder-ness to stare at you across the Portneuf River, and Bersimis was at least forty miles beyond. One visitor had followed the tele-graph line through bush. The only boat to make calls, slowing up off the village once or twice a month, started from a port far down the opposite shore. In winter government planes brought mail and attended to emergencies. The best way to get there would be to hire a fishing boat or heavy launch somewhere be-yond the Saguenay.

There were also permits to be secured, for the village was protected by the government. Once there, however, I would see something of Algonquin life, for the Montagnais of Bersimis were probably the largest Indian tribal group left anywhere in the high Northeast. They were descendants of the hunting, nomad tribes who had once held the wild country to the north of the St. Lawrence, often venturing far westward through the bush. The community was still a part of early nineteenth-century Indian life; in the twentieth, it lived by the fur trade. The Indians arrived on the river in early summer and spent two or three months at Bersimis in quarters built for them by the government. At Bersimis they made their contact with religion and civilization, got married in church, had their children bap-tized, attended to their religious duties and sold their furs. At the close of the short northern summer each family group packed its canoe with flour, tea, lard and ammunition and returned to the bush above the height of land. Here the tribe dispersed, breaking up into family bands in the ancient Algonquin manner, each band having its own hunting and trapping area. They lived in the bush in shelters or tents, and there was often only a wall of canvas between the newborn child and the arctic gale.

When spring—which is the bad, the hated, season in the woods—had come to an end with its mud and rotten ice, and the tributary rivers were free, the families came out of the woods in their canoes, each with its bale of pelts. Sometimes the luck had been good and they soon had money to spend; sometimes the luck had been bad, and men, women and children had a thin time. Some families had better luck than others. The aged and the ill were left behind at Bersimis, where the sisters wintered them in a sort of hospital-home and also kept a school. The Eudist fathers were in charge of the parish, and the resident government agent—by a convention frequent in Canada—was also a physician.

The tribe was large, and there were sometimes five or six hundred Indians in the summer community. They kept one great annual feast and celebration, the Feast of the Assumption of the Virgin, which falls on August fifteenth. The celebration marked the traditional date of the return to the woods. Paddling from the St. Lawrence into the brown wash of the Betsiamites, the people had set out together in a fleet, and there had been shouting and calling out of goodbyes till they turned a headland of the lesser river. Almost a year would elapse before they would be seen again, places empty in some canoes, and the children in arms staring at the red church tower and the beach.

One knows nothing whatever about a people until one has seen a number of them together. A common consciousness has to come into being before any group is free to act in its own pattern and mood. The first Indian I saw was watching us land at the

wharf. Indian villages are apt to include a native comic or ac-
knowledged jester, and I judged this first Indian to be the man.
He was short, hardly taller than a stocky boy just out of grammar
school, and his alert eyes were full of mischief and curiosity in
his brown Indian face. Taking us all in, he tossed a disconnected
word or two of French upon the air, all by way of identification of
us, greeting, and humor. Whites seldom apprehend the Indian
capacity for humor, for elfish, often ironic, fun. They are thoroughly capable, for instance, of "playing Indian" exactly like
small boys when they feel that it is expected of them by visiting
whites. I found later in the day that I was not mistaken in my
identification. This was the Tyll Eulenspiegel of the tribe.

The last population of Indians I had seen gathered into a
large community had been that of a pueblo on the Rio Grande.
I remembered a morning in the spring, a great dance before a
row of cottonwoods, and the strange, yet curiously beautiful,
orange-brown color of the smooth half-naked bodies crouching and treading to the ritual measure of the drum. Here in
the north, the forest made for no such color or sleekness. Passing us by in the early afternoon, coming towards us between
their unpainted shacks, the Algonquin Montagnais turned to
us faces as dark brown as dark, old-fashioned, plug tobacco. The
eye, again, was brown, but of a deep and lively glisten, having
nothing of that obsidian remoteness which can be stony in the
West. As a people, they were neither tall nor short, but of a
certain lean, well-proportioned middle height, and they walked
with the Indian assurance which has its roots in the old connection with the earth. Now and then, stockier, heavier types
brought out the more conventional spareness. The clothes were
simply habitant French Canadian—slouch hat, blue windbreaker
jacket and bottes sauvages. A few were wearing new-looking
woolen shirts of the large black-and-white and red-and-black
checks popular in the north. The women, however, more conservative, had retained something Indian and characteristic. It

194

was the picturesque and handsome Montagnais squaw hat, a kind of modified liberty-cap affair, cut full at the bottom like a bag and narrowing to a somewhat mounded top. To make it, tapering segments of broadcloth, alternately red and black, had been sewn together to a peak which was worn falling over towards the forehead. Around the base, looking very Chinese, ran a decorative piping of colored silks very finely rolled together—a Montagnais handicraft. The hair was worn in a kind of roll over the ear, the arrangement just showing below the edge of the hat.

The beginnings of such a hat are surely European in their inspiration—for the first Montagnais had no cloth—but the Indian mind has made the design its own and the whole effect is ritual and Asiatic. It has nothing whatever to do with Cartier or Champlain, but much to do with Marco Polo and the Grand Chan. Adding to the effect was the power and dignity of the faces of many of the older women. The patient, dark, Asiatic visages were not "beautiful" in the formal and European sense of the word, but they had that compensation of age in a primitive society, a look of character and realized authority.

One could tell the worldly circumstances of a family by the look of the dogs outside the door. Where the family had done well at its hunting and trading, the dogs looked comfortable; where the family was hard put to it, the dogs had the household's lean and hungry air. The board houses had a kitchen and a bedroom and were furnished with few things. In a kitchen you would find a small wood range, a table, a chair or two, a dish or two, an iron pot, a devotional calendar, and scarce another item of property. The list, perhaps, sounds barren, but one felt nowhere a need of things. The rooms were neat, and there was a complete naturalness and ease in the austerity. But I must not forget the bit of caribou hide which served so many as a mat, nor the home-mounted caribou horns with the one old hat hanging from a prong.

In front of the presbytery stood a garden walled about with

195

straggling wire. It was August and the short summer really over, but there were raspberries still waiting to be picked in the enclosure, one last grim rose, and noble clumps of aconite in early flower. As I sat alone on the presbytery steps in the dusk, staring down into the garden, and fending off the wilderness mosquitoes, there came towards me from behind the presbytery two Indian men. One was in old blue clothes and high boots, the other in old clothes more greyish, and I thought them both to be younger men in the thirties. Some sort of strange motion and scuffle as of dogs, yet not quite doglike, was going on behind them, and I presently saw that the visitor in blue had with him two bear cubs on a long chain borrowed from a trap. The little bears were both fretful and mischievous, weaving about and pulling back, but the Indian leader chivvied them along, and I saw him fasten the pair to a post of the presbytery stairs. The visitors then came over to me, and seeing that they wished to speak, I made signs to them to join me on the steps, and so we sat close together in the dusk. Their faces were very dark and Indian above the poorish European clothes, but they were not, thank God, smashed men, and the look on their youngish faces was unhaunted and completely natural. The bear-leader began by speaking into his companion's ear a long sentence in Montagnais. When this interesting and mysterious communication had come to its end, the companion turned his head to me and translated the message into easy French.

"The chief has come to make you welcome," he said. "He is glad you have come to visit us and hopes you will stay."

"Tell the chief I thank him very much," I said (and here I translate my French reply). "A stranger will long remember such a welcome in his heart. Tell him that I have heard of him and of his people, and am glad to be with them at Bersimis."

This seemed to please them, and we parted with an old-fashioned and pleasantly ceremonial politeness which was both

Indian and French. (It was the beginning of a friendship.) Standing on the steps, I watched them unloose their cubs, and turn the corner of the house. In their winterish clothes, the visitors melted swiftly into the night. It had grown cold and dark.

[From "Wildlife of the Stream"]

I had once a memorable glimpse upon the river of that image as it sometimes reveals itself to the human spirit. I was in a small boat, a kind of fisherman's launch, chugging eastward to the Indian settlements a full forty miles beyond the Saguenay. We stood inshore to make the journey, the last farms and villages falling astern as we ploughed ahead, the empty wilderness succeeding, sunlit near by and ominous beyond with dark gatherings of cloud. Fir trees, short and twisted and drawn up thick on a gigantically broken and rocky shore, passed us by for miles, the seas booming and leaping in this wild confusion, and breaking with a shatter of water and light on ledges scattered ahead. Early in the afternoon, the sunlight took on a cloudy glow, and in a few swift minutes there was a sudden pandemonium of furious and blinding rain. Then followed the veiled sun and the rain together, and presently the sun stood free in a great window of the storm.

There was vapor below—such vapor as follows rain at sea—and vapor sailing overhead; the sun again appeared, and all about us the St. Lawrence came into the restored light rain-lashed with trailing spume and foam. A mystery of color began to glow about us, touching the near land and the foam-running waves; we were in the magical world of the rainbow's end. Staring out into the colored sea, we presently found ourselves a part of a divine fantasy, inhabitants of the fabulous isle of Ariel and Prospero. Into that color which was air and light came the white whale.

197

Passing close by, a school tumbled and plunged in its huge gaiety, the glistening white bodies glowing with the beautiful, the enchanted, light, and wheeling over the delicate glowing on the foam. They passed and were gone, and the rainbow was in a little while as though it had never been, but the sun lingered, the storm piling up dark on the edge of the world like the tempest of Ariel's contriving—all else the St. Lawrence, the wilderness and the rock and a heavier sound of waves from the ancient chaos of the shore.

Publisher's Acknowledgments

SOUTH OF MAINE

This section includes passages from *The Outermost House* by Henry Beston. Copyright 1928, 1949, © 1956 by Henry Beston. Reprinted by permission of Holt, Rinehart and Winston, Inc.

IN MAINE

This section includes passages from the following books: *White Pine and Blue Water* by Henry Beston. Copyright © 1950 by Henry Beston. *Herbs and the Earth* by Henry Beston. Copyright 1935, © 1963 by Henry Beston. Reprinted by permission of David R. Godine. *Northern Farm* by Henry Beston. Copyright 1948 by Henry Beston. Reprinted by permission of Holt, Rinehart & Winston, Inc. *American Memory* by Henry Beston. Copyright 1937, © 1965 by Henry Beston.

"Sound and Life," by Henry Beston, was in the Contributors' Club of *The Atlantic Monthly* for January 1933. "Great Realities" is from April 5, 1956, Farm and Home Week banquet program, the College of Agriculture, University of Maine, Orono. "Farm Breakfast," October 24, 1939, "Aquarius," March 11, 1940; "The Young Philosopher's Song," September 5, 1940; and "To a Small Comic Dog," February 18, 1941, copyrighted in the respective years shown by *The Christian Science Monitor*. Reprinted by permission.

NORTH OF MAINE

This section includes passages from *The St. Lawrence* by Henry Beston. Copyright 1942 by Henry Beston. Copyright © 1970 by Elizabeth Coatsworth Beston.

About the Author

HENRY BESTON, born in 1888 in Quincy, Massachusetts, spent what he called "a New England boyhood of sea and shore, enriched with a good deal of the French spirit, from a French mother." He graduated from Harvard in 1909, received his M.A. there in 1911, and taught a year in France at the University of Lyon. In World War I, he served on land and later in the navy, in submarines, and wrote several books about the war. He was the editor of *Living Age* magazine before he dedicated himself to being a writer-naturalist and began work on *The Outermost House*, published in 1928. In 1929 he married Elizabeth Coatsworth and three years later moved his family to Chimney Farm in Nobleboro, Maine, where he lived until his death in 1968.

About the Editor

ELIZABETH COATSWORTH, born in Buffalo, New York, in 1893, was graduated from Vassar College, received her M.A. from Columbia University, and was awarded doctoral degrees from the University of Maine and New England College for her contribution to American letters. She was the author of many books, including books for children, novels, essays, short stories, and poetry—always her favorite form. She lived in Maine and wrote about Maine, living in the old farmhouse at Chimney Farm she and her husband bought after the publication of *The Outermost House*.